C000261816

THE
LAMDA GUIDE
TO
ENGLISH LITERATURE

OBERON BOOKS
LONDON

First published by Oberon Books Ltd (incorporating Absolute Classics), 521 Caledonian Road, London N7 9RH, in association with the London Academy of Music and Dramatic Art, Tower House, 226 Cromwell Road, London SW5 0SR.

Copyright The London Academy of Music and Dramatic Art © 1997

All rights reserved. No reproduction, copy or transmission of this publication may be made without written permission.

No paragraph of this publication may be reproduced, copied, or transmitted save with written permission or in accordance with the provisions of the Copyright, Designs and Patents Act 1988, or under the terms of any license permitting limited copying issued by the Copyright Licensing Agency, Concept House, Cardiff Road, Newport, South Wales, NP9 1RH.

Any person who does any unauthorised act in relation to this publication may be liable to criminal prosecution and civil claims for damages.

This book is sold subject to condition that it shall not by way of trade or otherwise be circulated without the publisher's consent in any form of binding or cover other than that in which it is published and without a similar condition including this condition being imposed on any subsequent purchaser.

ISBN   1 84002 011 3

Cover design: Andrzej Klimowski

Typography: Richard Doust

CONTENTS

THE NINETEENTH CENTURY NOVEL

Scott, Austen, Gaskell, the Brontës, Thackeray, Dickens, Trollope, Eliot, Collins, Marryatt, Reade, Meredith, Butler, Pater, Wilde, Hardy, Webb, James, Conrad

DRAMA 1800-1914

Robertson, Boucicault, Ibsen, Strindberg, Chekhov, Wilde, Shaw, Jones, Granville-Barker, Barrie, Galsworthy, Pinero, Yeats, Synge

THE TWENTIETH CENTURY NOVEL

Kipling, Forster, Galsworthy, Bennett, Maugham, Wells, Joyce, Woolf, Lawrence, Huxley, Priestley, Orwell, Waugh, Peake, Bowen, Compton-Burnett, Goudge, Greene, K. Amis, Durrell, Golding, Powell, Murdoch, Spark, Storey, Sillitoe, Barstow, Hines, Burgess, Scott, James, Rendell, Vine, M. Amis, Ackroyd, Rushdie, Ishiguro, Atwood, Boyd, Brookner, Byatt, Drabble, Du Maurier, Fowles, Garner, Horwood, Hill, Isherwood, O'Brien, Okri, Pym, Renault, St Auban de Terain, Theroux, Tremain, Wesley, White, Hulme, Keneally, Camus, Colette, Eco, Moravia, Nabokov, Sartre, Faulkner, Fitzgerald, Hemingway, Mailer, Morrison, Roth, Salinger, Vidal, Walker

TWENTIETH CENTURY POETRY

Yeats, Owen, Thomas, Brooke, Rosenberg, Sassoon, Graves, Bridges, Eliot, Auden, Day-Lewis, Spender, MacNeice, Muir, Lawrence, Peake, Amis, Durrell, D. Thomas, Larkin, Hughes, Plath, Smith, Gunn, Betjeman, Patten, McGough, Henri, Jennings, Roethke, R. S. Thomas, Wain, Harrison, McGluckian, O'Neill, Hesketh, Fuller, Middleton, Porter, Merwin, MacBeth, Barker, Campbell, cummings, Drinkwater, Empson, Frost, Lowell, Masefield, Moore, Nash, Pound, Sansom, Sitwell, Tate

TWENTIETH CENTURY DRAMA

O'Casey, Maugham, Priestley, Coward, Sherriff, Lonsdale, Rattigan, Eliot, Auden, Isherwood, Fry, Osborne, Beckett,

Delaney, Bolt, Jellicoe, Arden, D'Arcy, Wesker, Shaffer, Pinter, Storey, Nichols, O'Neill, Williams, Miller, Albee, Shepard, Mamet, Guare, Whiting, Simpson, Livings, Bond, Orton, Hare, Poliakoff, Griffiths, Brenton, Barker, Keefe, Edgar, Stoppard, Ayckbourn, Clark, Kempinski, Medoff, Kramer, Kushner, Bennett, Friel, Russell, Hampton, Wertenbaker, Churchill, Page, Gems, Daniels, Cartwright, Berkoff, Frayn, Gray, Godber, Harwood, Lowe, Lucie, Nicholson, Roche, Whitemore

INTRODUCTION

This guide is a revised edition of the original *LAMDA Guide to English Literature* by Bernard Brixey, which was first published by the Academy in 1984. Bernard Brixey sadly died in 1992, after a long and distinguished career. He made a lifelong study of language, literature and philosophy and, among many other achievements, wrote his own version of *The Oresteia* of Aeschylus.

This edition updates and reorganises the original *Guide*. Like that publication, this is essentially an overview of the development of English literature, designed to be of particular use for students studying for the LAMDA Licentiate Teacher's Diploma. It may be read either as an introduction to the subject, or as an extended reading list.

If used as a reading list, the authors and titles printed in **bold** type are the key writers and works in the development of English literature. Other titles and authors, which may be read for a more thorough appreciation of a writer and his period, are printed in normal type.

It would also be a good idea to accompany your reading with a modicum of history. Penguin publish a thorough, if sometimes dry, historical overview of Britain's past.

Bernard Brixey held many strong views, as do I. You may find this guide "partial, prejudiced and ignorant," as Jane Austen described herself. This is no bad thing. It is worth remembering that there are no "right answers" when it comes to the appreciation of literature. One of Bernard's maxims was, "Don't read books about literature, read the literature itself," a sentiment with which I wholeheartedly concur.

This edition is dedicated to the memory of Bernard Brixey, a valued friend of the Academy and an examiner of many years service.

Shaun McKenna
January 1997

THE MIDDLE AGES

CHAUCER AND HIS CONTEMPORARIES

A rich Anglo-Saxon literature stretches as far back as the eighth century but it cannot be understood by modern readers without special study. An idea of the subject matter, the sensitivity and the mystery of Anglo-Saxon literature can be gleaned by the modern reader by attempting a translation of *Beowulf,* published in paperback by Penguin.

A combination of factors virtually destroyed Anglo-Saxon – the Norman conquest, the subsequent internecine struggles between barons and kings, the development of the feudal system and the declaration that Norman French be the official language of the country. Anglo-Saxon became a hybrid tongue with no grammar, poor syntax and impossible spelling. However, Norman rulers found it necessary to learn some Anglo-Saxon in order to command their serfs, and the conquered had perforce to learn some rudimentary Norman French to satisfy their masters. As a consequence, during the years between the Conquest and c1300, a "new" language slowly began to emerge, which today we call Middle English.

The Normans had brought with them both Latin and a well-developed French culture. This brought a clarity of thought and expression into the language, whereas Anglo-Saxon had been prosaic and practical, with a mixture of mystery and imagination derived from the Celtic lands of Wales and Ireland. Since this time there has always been a creative tension in English literature between clarity on the one hand, and mystery and imagination on the other.

By the fourteenth century, grammatical and syntactical Middle English was beginning to be taught in the grammar schools just at the time that **GEOFFREY CHAUCER** (1340-1400) began his studies.

Chaucer is the first great English writer. Like Shakespeare after him, Chaucer was in the right place at the right time. He occupied a persuasive position in society. He was a courtier and special emissary of the King, twice ransomed from captivity in Europe whilst on royal missions.

Various dialects were spoken in different parts of the country, often very different from each other. Northumbrian, for example, could not be readily understood in the South, and vice versa. The Middle English that Chaucer used and developed was a mixture of East Midland and Southern dialects, sometimes called London English. To this he brought a knowledge and experience of Latin, and the French and Italian writers he met on his travels through Europe.

Middle English was promulgated in 1362 as the official language of the country, in place of Norman French. It is not the same as Modern English but it is sufficiently akin to it for the modern reader to understand it with a little effort. The new language depended on the order of words in the sentence; the constant, wearing alliteration of Old English was modified; and the heavy consonants of the old gave way to the vowels, rhythms and assonances of the new.

Chaucer's work developed in three periods. He began by writing allegorical verse in the French manner, using octo-syllabic couplets, as in *The Romaunt of the Rose*. He wrote in seven line stanzas, which were much influenced by the work of the Italian writers, Dante, Petrarch and Boccaccio. *The House of Fame* and **Troylus and Cryseyde** (at least some of which should be attempted) are works from this fruitful period. His final period, and the period of his greatness, saw Chaucer writing in a wide variety of styles – chivalrous, moralising, burlesque, magical and fabulous. His key work is **The Canterbury Tales**, an unfinished collection of stories (in the manner of Boccaccio's *Decameron*) supposedly told by a group of pilgrims on their journey from London to the shrine of St Thomas Becket at Canterbury. The tales vary from the sombre, almost sadistic **Knight's Tale** to the unbridled rumbustiousness and vulgarity of **The Miller's Tale, The Merchant's Tale** and **The Wife of Bath's Prologue and Tale**. Other contrasting tales which should be read for a full taste of the work are *The Pardoner's Tale* (which includes the saying "the love of money is the root of all evil"), *The Clerk's Tale* and the charming fable of Pertelot, Chanticleer and Reynard the Fox in *The Nun's Priest's Tale*.

The tone of *The Canterbury Tales* is enormously varied – amusing, tolerant, cheerful, tender, and ironic. The contrast between what characters actually do and what they *ought*to do is wittily underlined. There is nothing cruel or harsh in Chaucer, only the irony of the human condition and occasionally a merciless mockery of individuals. He never seems to hate anyone, even the most despicable, though his criticism can be biting. Cole's Notes publish a serviceable translation of *The Prologue* with the original Middle English on the left hand page and the translation line by line on the right hand page. But try to read some of the original to savour the flavour and sound of it and the ease with which Chaucer wrote. If you decide to memorise some for speaking, then consult the Penguin translation of the entire work by E.V. Rieu and there is a witty, if idiosyncratic, translation by Neville Coghill.The *Tales* are easier to read in the original than the *Prologue.*

At the end of the seventeenth century, John Dryden saw Chaucer as a innovator, "the father of modern English poetry." A few years later, Alexander Pope regarded Chaucer and Dryden as each bringing order out of chaos in their respective periods, imposing authority and laying the groundwork for the further development of the English language and its literature.

Contemporaries of Chaucer rarely attain his stature, though there was a considerable amount of other writing. Religious works and sermons appeared, as did stories of King Arthur's Court and GEOFFREY OF MONMOUTH's *History of Kings of Britain.* Many lyric poems, too, were written such as *Sumer is Icumen In.* In general, the verse of the period is more effective than the prose, which is of a poor quality, only gradually developing its syntax.

WILLIAM LANGLAND (c1330-1400), JOHN GOWER (c1330-1408), JOHN WYCLIFFE (c1320-1384) and the anonymous author of both *Pearl* and *Sir Gawain and the Green Knight* are all worth investigating. Langland's authorship of *Piers Plowman* has been questioned by some modern critics but that does not detract from its fine quality, alliterative in the old style. John Gower's *Confessio Amantis* is a collection of tales written in octo-syllabic lines and John Wycliffe is best known as the initiator of the translation of the Bible into English. Read a little of each writer and you will see how, good as they are, Chaucer towers above them all.

THE FIFTEENTH AND EARLY SIXTEENTH CENTURIES

The years between 1400 and 1500 saw literature stagnate. Writing was largely in imitation of Chaucer, but by writers without his qualities. Historically it was a tumultuous period, with Bolingbroke's usurpation of the crown from Richard II and the consequent "Wars of the Roses". These involved a total of eight kings and countless nobles, until Henry VII began the reign of the Tudor dynasty at the Battle of Bosworth Field. These years are commemorated in Shakespeare's history plays, though not always accurately and from a Tudor standpoint. Such events did not create a climate in which great writing was possible.

However, the ballads of the period are worth attention. Ballads were generally written in rhyming couplets of seven iambics, but set out as four-line stanzas of alternate four and three iambics because they are easier to print that way. Usually adventurous stories, the ballads go with a swing and are easy to memorise and to speak. To get the feel of them try reading *Sir Patrick Spens, Chevy Chase, The Nut-Browne Mayde, The Battle of Otterburn* and *Edward, Edward* (the last quite sophisticated). There are so many extant ballads that practically every anthology contains some. The ballad form caught the imagination of authors and public alike and has been imitated ever since - see some of the *Robin Hood Ballads,*

The Rime of the Ancient Mariner (Coleridge), *La Belle Dame Sans Merci* (Keats) and *The Diverting History of John Gilpin* (Cowper).

The prose of these years is not good. SIR THOMAS MALORY (died 1471) is justly famous for his *Morte D'Arthur* (not to be confused with Tennyson's poem), which is probably the best writing of the period and should be sampled, for it has impressive passages. WILLIAM CAXTON established the first English Press in 1477. This helped to discipline the language, and began to formalise vocabulary, spelling and punctuation.

Drama in England first took coherent shape around 1100 and by the fifteenth century the MYSTERY, MIRACLE and MORALITY plays were widely performed. For the origin of drama we must move back into antiquity, to the primitive village life of man. The day that the first medicine man adopted a special make-up or costume and "performed" before a group of villagers was the day on which drama began. Richard Southern in *The Seven Ages of the Theatre* has traced the development of primitive theatre right up to the full secular INTERLUDE of Medieval England, which itself developed into the play form we know today.

MIRACLE PLAYS arose initially in the church. The Mass itself, apart from its religious significance, is a highly dramatic liturgy. Chants alternating between priest and congregation by acting out Bible stories often contained ritualistic movement and gesture. Priests must have noticed the popularity of secular interludes. Illiterate Anglo-Saxons could not read the scriptures, so priests took to the altar steps after Mass to teach the congregation by acting out Bible stories. They evidently enjoyed the playlets, for the presentations got a little out of hand and were banned by the Pope. They were then taken outside to the porch steps. The Pope stopped that, too, so they moved to platforms in the local inn-yard. Soon they were performed anywhere there was a large enough space – the market place, even the streets. The earliest Miracle Play seems to have been *Ludus de Saint Katherina*, as early as 1100.

Away from the church, the plays soon expanded, introducing much more comedy, often of a bawdy nature. They were subsequently taken over by the Craft Guilds, presented on wagons called "Pageants". York, Chester, Wakefield and Coventry have famous cycles. *Noyes Fludde* belongs to the *Chester Cycle* and *Adam* is one of the earliest. Both are available and should be looked at.

MORALITY PLAYS came later, especially in the fifteenth and sixteenth centuries. They were didactic in tone, teaching little moral lessons but with plenty of comedy to sweeten the pill. Abstract characters like Perseverance, Avarice and Hypocrisy appear frequently. INTERLUDES continued as short, farcical breaks between the more serious Moralities, the most famous being the humorous *The Three Ps*. The best known Moralities are probably *The World and the Child* and *Everyman*, both of which should be read. *Everyman* is still presented today. Perhaps the most accessible way to approach the plays of this period is to read Tony Harrison's celebrated version of *The Mysteries* presented by the National Theatre in the early 1980s.

Professional actors were employed for the first time in the late fifteenth century, eventually forming themselves into companies (such as The Merchant Taylors' Company) to give them some respectability. The Merchant Taylors' Company performed occasionally at court, in barons' castles and in the towns.

Despite Chaucer and his many imitators, the new language ran into difficulties. Constantly but cautiously developing, it was beset with problems of rhyme, rhythm, accent, inflection and syntax. Even Caxton's printing press failed to halt a decline, and there was no great writer to take command.

There are no great literary figures of the fifteenth century, only scholars and translators. SIR THOMAS MORE (1478-1535) is probably the only name popularly remembered, and that more for the manner of his death than for his writings. He produced *Utopia* in Latin in 1517. The book outlines an ideal state although the title itself is Greek for "no place at all." It may well have been written ironically since More was a staunch Roman Catholic, executed for maintaining his religious beliefs after the institution of the Church of England. WILLIAM TYNDALE (1484-1536) and MILES COVERDALE (1488-1568) between them completed the translation of the Bible into English in 1535. *The Book of Common Prayer* was compiled by THOMAS CRANMER in 1549.

THE ENGLISH RENAISSANCE

THE ELIZABETHANS

The most important movement in the history of literature and art began in Italy, but took several years to really affect the English, largely because of the Reformation.

The Renaissance was fuelled by the rediscovery of the classical (ancient Greek and Roman) writers, whose work had been unknown for many centuries. 1453 might be taken as the key year, when the Turks captured Constantinople and drove refugee scholars to Italy. They took with them many lost texts – particularly the ancient Greeks: Homer, Plato, Aristotle, Aeschylus, Sophocles, Euripides and Zeno among them.

Between 1490 and 1520 this "rebirth" of classical thought influenced Europe enormously. It broadened people's minds, opened up a new world of thought and activity, and caused individuals to look into themselves. The result was a freeing of the sense of individuality, emphasising the dignity of individual rather than group personalities.

For a thousand years, the Church had taught its followers to look outside themselves to the practices and faith of Christianity as a sufficient consolation for their sufferings. Now, it became clear, other religions existed besides Christianity, and the teachings of the Greek philosophers and dramatists in search of Beauty, Truth and Goodness were attractive, serene and tolerant.

This is not the place to discuss the enormity of the Renaissance. Readers should consult an encyclopaedia or a Dictionary of Literary Terms to acquaint themselves with the changes wrought by it. Suffice it to say here that this release of energy, and broadening of knowledge, attitudes and speculation substantially influenced the creativity of the coming Elizabethan/Jacobean age, and its influence has lasted until today.

SIR THOMAS WYATT (1503-1542) and the EARL OF SURREY (1517-1547) though historically largely within the reign of Henry VII are 'Elizabethan' in tone. Both must be looked at for their introduction of the Petrarchan sonnet form from Italy. This was the octave-sestet (8-line 6-line) form, which had certain difficulties for the English vocabulary. Wyatt brought harmony and dignity to English verse. Surrey introduced new metrical devices taken up by later poets. Try Wyatt's *Forget Not Me, The Appeal* and *A Revocation*, three short poems respectively urging his mistress not to forget his steadfastness, not to forsake him, then, sadly, to bid her farewell. Try also his *To His Lute.* Of Surrey read *Description of Spring* and *Complaint of the Absence of Her Lover.*

Elizabeth ascended the throne in 1558. With the social changes that accompanied her reign began one of the most fertile periods in English literature.

The greatest poet of the period, aside from the dramatists, was **EDMUND SPENSER** (1552-1599). His work is ornate and full of the 'conceits' of the period, which sometimes make it heavy-going today without additional study. However, his importance cannot be over-estimated. *The Shepheard's Calendar* (1579) shows his love of nature and the earth. His attitude to life is expressed in *Hymns to Love and Beauty* (c 1570) which he said were written in "the greener times of my youth." For Spenser the love of woman reflected Divine Love, "virtue made visible."

The Faerie Queene (1591) is his best-known work, an epic seeking to teach "the art of living righteously." The characters are barely-developed, intellectual abstractions rather than real people, but the purity of the writing is rare and subtle. He invented his own stanza, the most difficult of all in English verse, consisting of nine lines, eight of five iambics and one of six, rhyming ABAB BCBC C, admirable for his purpose. English has always suffered from a limited number of rhymes, yet Spenser's rhyming is accomplished and effective. The work is incomplete, only six of the intended twelve books plus two cantos of the seventh were written. (A 'canto' is simply a division of a long poem, from the Latin *cantus-canere* = 'to sing'.)

The poem celebrates Gloriana, an idealised personification of Queen Elizabeth I, who holds a twelve-day feast. Each of the planned twelve books was to record the adventure of one of her knights, extolling one of the Virtues. As almost always with epics, the first two books are the best. The *Den of Mammon* and the *Temptation of Sir Guyon* in Book Two are the most impressive passages and the famous allegory of the *Cave of Despair* in Book Three is poignant.

SIR PHILIP SIDNEY (1554-1586) wrote some attractive songs and love sonnets in *Astrophel and Stella*, which are said to express his love for Lady Penelope Devereux. As well as being a poet of charm and sophistication, he wrote a major prose work – ***Apologie for Poetrie***, one of the first English analyses of the art of poetry, which should be read in order to compare it with those of Dryden and Shelley. In this instance 'Apologie' means a defence or justification, rather than the modern meaning. Sidney was the first poet to modify the Petrarchan sonnet (octet and sestet, see above) into the 'English' or 'Elizabethan' form of three quartets and a rhyming couplet, which was later used by Shakespeare.

MICHAEL DRAYTON (1563-1631) produced a vast quantity of verse, much of which is now largely forgotten. His sonnet *A Farewell* is remarkably modern and touching, and some of his *Poems Lyric and Pastoral* are worth attention.

In prose, SIR FRANCIS BACON (1561-1626) must be mentioned for his influence on the future of the language. He was not a 'literary' person in the accepted sense, but a brilliant lawyer whose reputation is that of a philosopher. His contribution to English was his demand for clear reasoning and precision, in contrast to the contemporary taste for imaginative and purely poetic language. The seventeenth century, largely because of the development of mathematical physics, has been recognised as the beginning of the modern, scientific world. Bacon was not a scientist, but he did recognise the coming of a new age and was full of faith in human progress. His accurate, lively style pushes the language towards a capacity for methodological and scientific analyses.

Bacon's best achievements are the *Essays* and *The Advancement of Learning*, the latter more direct, lively and enjoyable to read. *New Atlantis* is another Utopian work which might usefully be read in conjunction with More's *Utopia*. Bacon's influence lasted until the Romantic period in the nineteenth century.

Bacon, like Shakespeare and Ben Jonson, straddles the period into the Jacobean age, so named after the Latin name (Jacobus) of James I, who succeeded Elizabeth in 1603. The work of the Jacobean period had a particular flavour which will be discussed below, and Bacon's later writings reflect this more sombre cast of thought.

The glory of Elizabethan literature is the first great flowering of drama. The earliest plays we know are *Ralph Roister Doister* (1566) by NICHOLAS UDALL and *Gammer Gurton's Needle* (1567) by WILLIAM STEVENSON. Both are farcical comedies with still-amusing moments, if an idiosyncratic grasp of dramatic structure.

There are two important and highly influential precursors of Shakespeare, both of whom helped to develop the language and structure of drama – JOHN LYLY (1544-1606) and **CHRISTOPHER MARLOWE** (1565-1593). Lyly and Marlowe belonged to a group known as The University Wits, said to meet regularly at the Mermaid Tavern off Cheapside. Other members of the group were THOMAS NASHE, ROBERT GREENE, THOMAS LODGE and GEORGE PEELE. All were educated at Oxford or Cambridge when those universities were flourishing and expanding under the influence of the Renaissance. The University Wits were highly censorious of the upstart, 'uneducated' Shakespeare whom they regarded as unable to construct an adequate play and of appealing always to the lower tastes of the public. Greene is noted for his attack on the young Shakespeare as an "upstart

crow beautified with our feathers," a mere "Johannes Factotum
in his own conceit... the only Shakescene in a country."

Lyly developed English comedy and firmly established
the place of prose in play writing, ready for Dryden later to
perfect. His plays are tedious and dramatically stilted, with
paper-thin characters, and he overdoes the alliteration and
other devices. However, *Campaspe* (1584) and *Endimion*
(1591) could be plodded through, largely because one begins
to see the developing tones that Shakespeare will use.

Marlowe is an altogether more sophisticated and
passionate dramatist, as well as having led a reputedly
exciting life. He is believed to have been a spy in
Walsingham's embryonic secret service, and was killed by
having a dagger driven through his eye into his brain,
reputedly in the Mermaid Tavern. Whether this was the result
of a drunken brawl or because of his underworld connections
is a subject richly disputed by historians and scholars. To
Marlowe goes the distinction of setting the style of verse
writing which Shakespeare was to develop into such an all-
encompassing and flexible form. Marlowe brought blank
verse (unrhymed lines of five iambics) to great heights, and
his best work drives along with a passionate urgency and
intensity. He is also the first English playwright to develop
three-dimensional characters.

Dr Faustus is his undoubted masterpiece. This was
published in two different editions. The 1605 is shorter and
more streamlined, while the 1616 edition includes some very
messy comedy scenes now usually printed in modern
editions. *Dr Faustus* deals with the legend of the scholar who
sells his soul to the Devil in return for twenty-five years of
power, which he wastes in hedonism. It has a magnificent
opening and ending, but the middle is not well-constructed.
Marlowe's other important plays are *Edward II*, a sympathetic
account of a weak monarch whose homosexual association
with Gaveston caused his downfall; *The Jew of Malta*, a blackly
comic – and to modern tastes deeply anti-Semitic – tale of an
unscrupulous villain; and the long, unwieldy two part epic

tragedy *Tamburlaine The Great,* which has passages of magnificent if grandiloquent poetry. These should certainly be sampled.

Marlowe was also an accomplished lyric and narrative poet. **The Passionate Shepherd To His Love** is a justly famous pastoral, and *Hero and Leander* contains passages of great sensuousness, wit and lyrical beauty.

Other interesting and often amusing Elizabethan dramatists are BEAUMONT & FLETCHER (*The Knight of the Burning Pestle*), THOMAS DEKKER (*The Shoemaker's Holiday*), THOMAS HEYWOOD (*A Woman Killed With Kindness*), and THOMAS KYD (*The Spanish Tragedy*).

SHAKESPEARE

So much has been written about **WILLIAM SHAKESPEARE** (1564-1616) that one is reluctant to add to the many thousands of words on the subject. What is so remarkable about his work is partly historical accident. He lived at a time when the drama had been successfully developed into an appropriate, if often formal, form. He also lived in an age of exploration, and he successfully explored the psyches of a wider range of individuals than any other writer before or since. The tension between the highly-structured form and the almost naturalistic sympathy for the inner life of his characters enabled him to push back the boundaries of drama to an unprecedented degree. His sense of dramatic structure improved as he wrote, and he stands as a model of economy and precision, both in his thoughts and his manner of expressing them.

Most authors can, with study, be identified as having a particular set of values which they bring to their work. Shakespeare is remarkable in that he never presents us with his own opinions in a character's mouth. He always writes the character from the character's own point of view, and the language and vocabulary of each individual is always coherent and consistent. His other remarkable innovation lies in his remarkable characterisations of women, something Marlowe certainly never achieved.

Of his life we know little. He was born in Stratford upon Avon on April 23rd 1564, eldest son and third child of John Shakespeare and his wife Mary, daughter of Robert Arden, a well-to-do local farmer. Shakespeare was educated at the free Stratford Grammar School and, in 1582, aged 18, married Anne Hathaway of Shottery. Their elder daughter, Susannah, was born the following year and they subsequently had another daughter, Judith, and a son, Hamnet, who died some time in the 1590s. William left Stratford in 1585 and went to London where he became acquainted with Lord Southampton, his principal patron. He seems to have worked in some capacity at one of the two London theatres (The Theatre and The Curtain) and subsequently became a member of the Lord Chamberlain's Men. We know that by 1592 Shakespeare was established as both an actor and a playwright, and he subsequently appeared in the first performances of two plays by his contemporary, Ben Jonson. The Lord Chamberlain's Men were led by James and Richard Burbage, the actor who created most of the great Shakespearian heroes, and by 1598 Shakespeare was sufficiently prominent to share in the establishment of the new Globe Theatre on the Bankside.

As well as writing plays, Shakespeare wrote a magnificent collection of *Sonnets,* mysteriously dedicated to 'Mr W.H.', clearly a wealthy and good looking young man whose identity is the subject of much scholarly and romantic debate. The identity of the 'Dark Lady' mentioned in the Sonnets has caused similar speculation. Of his other poems, *Venus and Adonis* and *The Rape of Lucrece* are both dedicated to Henry Wriothesley, Earl of Southampton, who is the most probable candidate for 'Mr W.H.' Had he not been a playwright, the *Sonnets* and passages of *The Rape of Lucrece* would have placed Shakespeare in the front rank of Elizabethan poets.

The plays fall into several periods:

The first, from c1590 to c1594, sees him experimenting with form and structure and developing the strong driving narrative of the history plays. Plays of this period include the three parts of *Henry VI*, **Richard III, The Taming Of The Shrew**, *Titus Andronicus*, **Romeo and Juliet**, *Two Gentlemen of Verona*, **The Comedy of Errors, Love's Labours Lost** and *King John*.

The second, from c1595 to c1600, sees the flowering of Shakespeare's genius, with many of the most popular plays. The plays of this period are lean, beautifully constructed, richer and deeper than those of the first period. This is the work of a man at the height of his powers. Plays include the two parts of **Henry IV, Richard II, A Midsummer Night's Dream, The Merchant of Venice, Much Ado About Nothing, Julius Caesar**, *The Merry Wives of Windsor*, **As You Like It, Twelfth Night** and *Hamlet*. These last three, particularly, show the start of the darkening of tone which was to characterise his work in the 1600s and which is, sometimes, romantically attributed to the death of his son.

The third period, from c1600 to 1608, is the period of the great, dark tragedies – **Othello, Antony and Cleopatra, Macbeth, Coriolanus** and *King Lear*. The comedies, too, take on very dark and sombre tones – **Measure For Measure, Troilus and Cressida**, *Timon of Athens* and *All's Well That Ends Well*. In these comedies there are few admirable or even likeable characters, and there is a desperation and cynicism that Shakespeare seems to be able to overcome in the tragedies. These are sometimes called "The Problem Plays", though the problems seem more often to be those of the critics than Shakespeare himself.

The final period, from c1609 to c1612, moves away from the darkness and the plays are fables of epic proportions, concerned with redemption and forgiveness – **The Winter's Tale**, *Cymbeline*, **The Tempest** and *Pericles*. The last play fully accepted into the canon, *Henry VIII*, is known to have been a collaborative effort with John Fletcher, and Shakespeare is also known to have contributed to two further plays, *The Two Noble Kinsmen* and *Sir Thomas More.*

Shakespeare retired to Stratford in 1611, where he built New Place and lived there until his death in 1616 at the age of 54. His daughters survived him, as did his widow to whom he left his 'second-best bed.' The plays were first collected in 1623 when the First Folio was put together by two actors from the Lord Chamberlain's Men (now renamed the King's Men), John Heminges and Henry Condell. Heminges is believed to be the actor who first played Falstaff.

Shakespeare had a remarkable vocabulary. Otto Jesperson in *The Growth and Structure of the English Language* gives him 21,000 words against Milton's 8,000 and the Old Testament's 4,800. The modern 'educated' person's has perhaps 2000, of which 700 are said to comprise the normal vocabulary of the average individual.

Shakespeare has not always been regarded as a great dramatist. There were times when he was considered very poor, even vulgar and crude, and both Dryden and Pope wrote 'improvements' of his plays. In the nineteenth century an editor called Thomas Bowdler cleaned up the bawdier moments in order to make them 'suitable' for family reading.

There is much to read and see of Shakespeare. Many of his speeches are, of course, well-known and countless lines have passed into everyday language. (One elderly lady once said that she did not like *Hamlet* very much because it was so full of quotations.)

THE JACOBEANS

The tone of the Jacobean period is extraordinarily dark and bitter. The closest modern analogy would be that of the German Expressionist movement in the first twenty years of the twentieth century. Interestingly, both preceded periods of violent social upheaval and change – in England the Civil War, in Germany the rise of the Nazis.

James I was a dour, secretive Scot, much given to interest in the occult and arcane subjects. He was a descendant of Banquo in *Macbeth* and there have been suggestions that Shakespeare wrote that play with an eye to flattering him. The best writing of the Jacobean age is the drama, and here we see a focus of interest on the seamy underbelly of society – on murder, madness, death, corruption and hypocrisy. The writers are, generally, sophisticated and passionate but the scope of the subject matter has narrowed since Shakespeare, becoming introspective. The Jacobean 'tragedies' are melodramas full of seething lust – for sex, money and power. The overriding image of society that one discovers here is one of sickness and moral lassitude. There are marvellous speeches and tremendously three-dimensional characters in these vivid and violent plays.

Some of the later Shakespeare plays (as one would expect from their period) foreshadow the masterpieces of Ford, Webster and Middleton. *Measure for Measure* and *Troilus and Cressida* clearly explore a world where morality has become secondary to expediency.

Revenge is a motive common to almost all the tragedies of the period, and to many of the comedies. The archetype is probably **CYRIL TOURNEUR**'s *The Revenger's Tragedy* (1607), a blackly comic tale which opens with our anti-hero holding the skull of his former fiancée and vowing a painful and lingering revenge on the Duke who first corrupted her and then caused her death. Tourneur is also sometimes credited with an interesting, if inferior, work, *The Atheist's Tragedy*.

There are three great playwrights of the period. **JOHN WEBSTER** (c1580-c1625) collaborated with several of his contemporaries on both comedies and serious plays, but his towering achievements are entirely his own work. *The Duchess of Malfi* (1614) and *The White Devil* (1608) show him at his best – dark, intense and full of character. Note his use of language and verse form. There are memorable characters: Vittoria Corombona, the White Devil herself, has some magnificent speeches, and the Duchess of Malfi's dignity in the face of appalling persecution by her lunatic brother is most moving. The Cardinal and Duke Ferdinand in *The Duchess* are fully realised characters: the latter's descent into madness as a result of his incestuous attraction towards his sister is most convincingly drawn. Both plays have their fair share of corpses, mysterious echoes, spies, madness, voyeurism, sadism and death.

THOMAS MIDDLETON (1570-1627) began his career by writing satirical comedies, also collaborating with such contemporaries as DEKKER, ROWLEY and MUNDAY. His 'city comedies', as they are now called, are blackly witty exposés of the pretensions and machinations of both the lower orders and the aristocracy. The best is probably *A Chaste Maid In Cheapside*, though *A Mad World My Masters, The Roaring Girl* and *A Trick To Catch The Old One* are all worth investigating. His final play, *A Game at Chess*, was a political satire which got him into trouble with the Privy Council. However, his twin masterpieces are tragedies – or more strictly, tragi-comedies. ***The Changeling*** tells the story of Beatrice-Joanna, a Spanish heiress who commissions an ugly groom, De Flores, to murder an unwelcome suitor. On successful completion of this task, De Flores demands Beatrice-Joanna's body as compensation. The developing sado-masochistic relationship between the two is startlingly drawn and psychologically complex. There is a subplot, mostly written by Rowley, about a woman wrongly incarcerated in a madhouse, which has few points of contact with the main plot. ***Women Beware Women*** tells of the corruption of the all-too-willing Bianca by the Duke of Florence, the forced marriage of Isabella to an idiot when she would prefer to sleep with her uncle, and an ageing high-born bawd who attaches herself to the estranged husband of Bianca. Almost all of them die during the final act in the course of a Masque – hidden spikes, poisoned incense and molten gold all feature as methods of destruction.

JOHN FORD (d 1639) was a Devon man whose work specialised in the depiction of sorrow, melancholy and despair.

This does not mean that the plays are not lively, however – quite the opposite. His most famous, *'Tis Pity She's A Whore*, tells of the incestuous love of Annabella for her brother Giovanni and its violent consequences. His other major plays are **The Broken Heart** and *Perkin Warbeck* and he collaborated with Dekker and Rowley on *The Witch of Edmonton*.

BEN JONSON

Jonson (1572-1637) firmly straddles both the Elizabethan and Jacobean periods and, while not exempt from the prevailing mood of either age, stands somewhat outside it. Like his contemporary, Donne (see below), he exerted considerable influence away from Shakespeare and towards the coming neo-classical age. It might be argued that these two heralded the coming of Milton and Dryden. Jonson was principally a dramatist, the antithesis of Shakespeare in that he was an admirer of classical order and perfection, seeking exact form, balance and accuracy in all he wrote. His satires (often very pointed), his epigrams, comedies and some fine lyrical poetry earn respect for his breadth of knowledge, strength of mind and dignity. His major plays are *Every Man in His Humour, Volpone* and **The Alchemist**, although in the latter he showed little knowledge of alchemy. These plays take great delight in exposing hypocrisy and sham. Jonson's language is intricate and ornate and his prevailing style somewhat cerebral and intellectual.

One of his most beautiful lyrics is *Queen and Huntress, Chaste and Fair* from *Cynthia's Revels* (Act V scene III), a masque written for the Court.

CAVALIERS, PURITANS AND THE AGE OF MILTON

This period between 1625 and 1649 is often referred to as the Caroline period, the reign of Charles I ('Caroline' from the Latin *Carolus*, = Charles).

Sir Francis Bacon had already pointed towards the coming developments in language. Cavaliers and Puritans now brought about a complete break with previous periods. With political upheavals, the rejection of Elizabethan ideals and the growing strength of Puritanism, the taste became one for critical and intellectual rather than emotional writing. Shakespeare and his contemporaries were rejected as coarse and unsophisticated.

The major political events of the period include the Civil War, the execution of Charles I and the establishment under Oliver Cromwell of the Commonwealth, when all theatres were closed by law. As always, periods overlap and the Restoration of Charles II in 1660 began a new period of literary endeavour. Some of the writers discussed below lived on into this "Age of Reason" but we may regard them as essentially Caroline for our purposes. Milton, for example, wrote and worked diligently for the Commonwealth but did not really achieve fame until after the Restoration. The Cavalier and Puritan poets are, in a sense, illustrative of the political split throughout England.

The Cavalier poets were much influenced by Ben Jonson. Their creativity is light, delicate, often expressed in perfectly-formed short poems. **ROBERT HERRICK**, THOMAS CAREW, EDMUND WALLER, SIR JOHN SUCKLING and RICHARD LOVELACE are the best known. A good anthology should contain selections from each of them. Herrick's *Daffodils* (which makes an interesting comparison with Wordsworth's later poem) and *Funeral Rights* are excellent examples of his work. Waller's

Old Age is worth looking at and Suckling's *The Constant Lover* and *Why so pale and wan?* have enormous charm. Lovelace's *To Althea from Prison* and *To Lucasta* are all short and attractive.

ANDREW MARVELL (1622-1678) was a gentle, happy man in his early years. He spent four years in Europe before becoming tutor to the daughter of Lord Fairfax at Nun Appleton in Yorkshire. His work shows a tender irony, self-mockery and a strong sense of the "deserts of vast eternity" to come in his seductive **To His Coy Mistress** and *The Definition of Love*. He took delight in nature, as shown in **The Garden** and *The Picture of Little T.C.*, an enjoyable group of poems by a likeable poet. *The Bermudas* is a beautiful song of praise and thanksgiving by a party of exiles approaching those islands, and in the celebrated **Horatian Ode Upon Cromwell's Return From Ireland** Marvell gives a very sympathetic and touching description of the execution of Charles I, unusual for a Puritan writer. The bulk of his work was not published until the 1680s.

The Puritan poets are better-known as the "Metaphysical Poets," of whom **JOHN DONNE** (1572-1631) is the most celebrated. They were more serious in tone than the Cavaliers, sometimes imbued with religious fervour. They get their name from their witty conceits and elaborate, often scientific, imagery. They were out of fashion until T. S. Eliot reappraised Donne during the early years of the twentieth century.

Donne, one of the key seventeenth century writers, began writing during the Jacobean part of Shakespeare's life and, like Bacon, had an enormous influence on literature and language. After the massive output of Elizabethan times, English had become a tired, cliché-ridden language needing something to give it fresh impetus. Highly intellectual, highly sensual and deeply religious, Donne fulfilled this function. He asserted that anything could be a fit subject for poetry, if realistically and maturely treated. He expected his reader to follow his quick mind and uncommon style. Poetry that would be new needed a new technique in presentation. His verse is characterised by the use of the famous 'conceit'. A conceit is simply an idea expressed in unexpected, often startling figurative terms. The use of fanciful metaphor and simile, intended to arrest, surprise and delight the reader by its wit and ingenuity, appeals to the mind rather than to the feelings.

> Marke but this flea, and marke in this,
> How little that which thou deny's me is;
> It suck'd me first, and now sucks thee,
> And in this flea, our two bloods mingled bee;

Dr Helen Gardner has defined a conceit as 'a comparison whose ingenuity is more striking than its justness... A comparison becomes a conceit when we are made to concede likeness while being strongly conscious of unlikeness.' The unlikeness is as important as the likeness, and the reader must have both in mind.

In 1615 Donne entered the Church, his sermons being numbered amongst the best of the century. He was much concerned with first and last things. Dryden later commented that 'he affects ... the metaphysick', a tag that stuck and labelled Donne the first of the Metaphysical Poets. Donne's influence paved the way for the subsequent work of Milton and Dryden. Of his *Songs and Sonnets* read **The Extasie, The Apparition, The Funeral, The Good-Morrow** and the very beautiful **Go, And Catche A Falling Star**. **A Nocturnal Upon St Lucy's Day** is one of the most moving poems of despair and loss in the language. On religious themes look at **A Valediction Forbidding Mourning**, the sonnets **Death Be Not Proud** and **Song: Sweetest Love, I Do Not Goe**.

What is surprising about Donne, when one considers that he was Dean of St Paul's, is the passionate eroticism of some of his poems, such as **The Sun Rising** and some of the *Elegies* and *Satires*.

Other metaphysical poets were **GEORGE HERBERT** (1593-1633), RICHARD CRASHAW, HENRY VAUGHAN and THOMAS TRAHERNE. Herbert's work, all religious in tone, is almost entirely included in one volume called *The Temple*. Try **Virtue, A Dialogue, The Forerunner** and **Love**, though having once discovered Herbert's compassion and subtlety you may wish to read more widely. Crashaw's *Wishes To His (Supposed) Mistress* and *Hymn to Saint Teresa* are both effective and enjoyable poems. Vaughan's *Peace, The World* and *The Night* and Traherne's *Shadows in the Water* further illustrate the metaphysical poets, spaced over nearly a hundred years. Metaphysical poetry is more an attitude of mind than anything else. Helen Gardner's exhaustive book *The Metaphysical Poets* (Penguin) covers thirty-eight of them and contains a splendid introduction.

Amongst prose writers, ROBERT BURTON, SIR THOMAS BROWNE, JEREMY TAYLOR and IZAAC WALTON ought to be mentioned and some of their work looked at. Burton's famous *Anatomy of Melancholy* (1621), Browne's *Religio Medici* (1643), Taylor's *Holy Living* and *Holy Dying* and, of course, Walton's *Compleat Angler* (1653) could be savoured for their styles.

JOHN MILTON (1608-1674) used to be regarded as our greatest poet. He is certainly an important writer of enormous power, but he has fallen out of fashion because of a certain sententiousness and monotony of tone. At his best, this reputation is unjustified. When he is not writing at full power, a little of Milton may go a long way. It is sonorous, ornate, Latinate and egotistical. Milton was a man of strong, dominating personality, entirely sure of himself. He ceased writing poetry for some twenty years in order to serve the Commonwealth, in the certain knowledge that when he returned to it he would write a masterpiece, which he did. Growing tired of his first wife, a disastrous marriage, he wrote a pamphlet advocating divorce. He seems torn by inner conflict between the attractions of the paganism of Ancient Greece and Rome and his inner certainty of the validity of Christianity. It has been said of him that 'he sought to combine the richness of classical learning (Renaissance) with the revival of deep religious feeling (the Reformation).' The result was **Paradise Lost**, the only completed epic in the English Language. His *Paradise Regained* is nothing like as effective.

Milton used the same blank verse form as Shakespeare but developed it so that it is impossible to mistake the one for the other. One immediately notices the considerable vocabulary; the invention of new words – adverbs and nouns made from adjectives, nouns from verbs; the introduction of archaisms and Latinisms, broadening the language to record the universal ideas he expounded. One can imagine Milton reorganising Heaven for God. The opening of *Paradise Lost* moves through five whole lines before the main verb is introduced, a device common throughout Milton's work and over which he had perfect control. Similes usually break down at the very point of their aptness but Milton could expand a simile to make it almost entirely apposite. He was a master of all forms of verse: his sonnets are sonorously superb, as notable as those of both Shakespeare and Wordsworth. He even tried his hand at imitating the Classical Greek playwrights.

Of the shorter poems, one should read **On the Morning of Christ's Nativity, L'Allegro, II Penseroso, Lycidas**, as well as twelve superb sonnets (particularly **Avenge Oh Lord, Thy Slaughtered Saints**), which are crystal clear in thought and theme. These early poems have sometimes earned Milton the reputation of being "the last of the Elizabethans," albeit with definite signs of the coming classicism. *Samson Agonistes* was an attempt to write a tragedy in the ancient Greek form, although Milton called it a Dramatic Poem, based on the story of Samson in The Book of Judges. Some of it should be read, perhaps the fourth and fifth episodes from line 1062 to the end. The fourth episode is an extended lyrical lament on Samson's mental anguish and the fifth Samson's destruction of the Philistine Temple at Gaza and the death of the occupants. The first two books of *Paradise Lost* are essential reading too and books IX and X if there is time. At the Great

Consult in Book II, observe Milton's accuracy in writing individual speeches appropriate to the characters, holding back Satan's address until the end. They are excellent passages for speaking aloud, for Milton had much experience of political harangues and the devices used by politicians to create maximum effect. Observe as well how Satan himself is a surprisingly fine and noble figure, his only sin that of disobedience to God. He is one of the outstanding figures in literature.

For a modicum of lighter relief read either *Comus* or *Arcades*, loosely called masques. These were spectacular entertainments, in rustic settings, simple in thought and action and with music, songs, dance and disguises. They were usually performed at Court or in the homes of the nobility, often with members of the family taking leading roles. Inigo Jones, the great architect, designed decorations and machinery for the special effects for many masques. Their very simplicity called for care in presentation. In Milton's hands they were really a form of pastoral poetry.

THE RESTORATION
AND THE AGE OF REASON

While Milton's greatest poems were written after the Restoration of Charles II in 1660, temperamentally he belongs to the earlier age. Charles brought with him from France the influence of that country's most brilliant literary period, that of Pascal, Corneille, Racine and Moliere, the latter three fine dramatists who were to greatly influence Restoration playwriting. Charles was a poor ruler, not interested in the harsh and bitter political and religious quarrels of the time, nor in the commercial wars between English and Dutch merchants. He preferred lighter entertainment. The Great Plague occurred in 1665 and a year later the Great Fire of London destroyed large areas of the city. Charles was followed by James II in 1685, a Catholic wishing to favour Catholics, appointing them to high office and thereby causing more squabbling between Catholics and Protestants. Parliament invited William and Mary of Orange to take over the throne in 1688. They accepted and James fled to France. So Parliament by a 'Bloodless Revolution' asserted its supremacy over the monarch.

The period is also referred to as the Classical Period or the Age of Reason. There is a great gulf between its own standards and those of earlier periods. Shakespeare, for instance, was considered ridiculous, even disgusting. The taste of this new period demanded reasoned, precise writing rather than the use of the imagination, as one would expect from the French influence. Samuel Butler, John Bunyan and John Dryden dominate the age, which also saw the establishment of the Restoration Theatre.

JOHN BUNYAN (1628-1688) is famous for *The Pilgrim's Progress*, the story of a Christian pilgrim's progress from the City of Destruction to the Celestial City, resisting the temptations of this world to save his soul for the next. One of the most widely-read books in literature, it was popular from the first, largely for its sincerity. Harking back to the

Puritan tradition, it contrasts with SAMUEL BUTLER (1612-1680) whose *Hudibras*, a mock-heroic poem in lines of eight syllables, satirises the Puritans Bunyan was so anxious to celebrate. Butler's verse is often little more than doggerel but it does illustrate the excesses of the Puritan period, so intent upon destroying the natural, human joy in life.

JOHN DRYDEN (1631-1700) stands above all his contemporaries, his work covering forty years. He imposed upon himself the tag, 'Be thou clear' and had an enormous influence on the writing of English. His ability to control language and thus to make his meaning exact enhanced the future of English writing, and his style was to be much imitated, especially by Pope. Perhaps Dryden's greatest qualities were his imagery, particularly aural imagery, and a keen ear for consonantal and vowel sounds and their juxtaposition. 'By the harmony of sounds we allure the soul,' he said, or as Pope put it, 'the sound must seem an echo of the sense', a style called 'imitative harmony'.

Dryden was English literature's first great satirist, calm, scornful but tolerantly good-humoured. *Absalom and Achitophel*, a highly political critique, answered the contemporary taste for criticism rather than new creative work. Dryden perfected the 'heroic couplet', destined to become the standard verse form of the eighteenth century. The term 'heroic couplet' refers originally to the dactylic hexameter used in ancient Greek literature but in English it is two rhyming pentameters, more suitable for English than the hexameter. It is used intellectually rather than for lyricism. Dryden eliminates all elisions, inversions, expletives and monosyllabic lines from his verse, and retains the monosyllable only for rhymes, to obtain the maximum stress. The regularities which he introduced led to the couplet having great dignity and power. Read *The Prologue of Aureng-Zebe*, the passage 'reason and religion' from *Religio Laici II* (noting sounds that create atmosphere), *Alexander's Feast, An Ode in Honour of St. Cecilia's Day* (which one wag called 'immortal ragtime') and some of another ode, *Song of St. Cecilia's Day*, beginning at "From harmony, from heavenly harmony". An ode was originally a song, but so many different forms have been used that the only appropriate definition is that an ode is written for a special occasion, in serious heightened language. Dryden's plays include the popular *Indian Emperor* (on Cortez' conquest of Mexico) and ***All for Love***, his version of the story of Antony and Cleopatra. This shows his appreciation of Shakespeare's merit, more clearly expressed in his ***Essay on Dramatick Poesie*** (to compare with those of Sidney and Shelley). His translation of Virgil's *Aeneid* contains many wonderful passages.

The famous diarists of the second half of the seventeenth century, JOHN EVELYN and SAMUEL PEPYS, should not be overlooked, nor the important philosophers THOMAS HOBBES (*Leviathan*) and JOHN LOCKE (*Essay Concerning Human Understanding*). Locke's simple, straightforward style also contributed to the development of prose writing in the following century.

Restoration Drama is well known, mainly for its comedies. This was a period in which largely the upper classes and fashionable society attended the theatre, and they loved to have their foibles and pretensions pointed out to them. Many of the earlier plays are extremely ribald, such as **WILLIAM WYCHERLEY**'s (1640-1716) ***The Country Wife***, and these 'high comedies' repay study. This was the period when the first actresses appeared in the theatre, female roles having hitherto been played by boys. Margaret Hughes, as Desdemona, was the first woman to appear on the London stage, and there were some interesting women playwrights – KATHERINE PHILIPS (known as 'The Matchless Orinthia') and **APHRA BEHN**, who was risqué even by the standard of the day. Behn's plays include *The Amorous Prince, The Dutch Lover* and ***The Rover***. Not only do these comedies reflect the times but, interestingly, serve as a barometer for the development of new moral standards.

Wycherley's play, along with his *The Plain Dealer*, is preoccupied with sexual desire at its most coarse and direct, wrapped up in wit and an ingeniously constructed plot. Wycherley, however, cannot disguise his objections to the new, freer morality of both men and women.

WILLIAM CONGREVE (1670-1729) is the finest of the Restoration dramatists, his masterpiece being *The Way of The World*, probably the finest high comedy in the language. *Love For Love* and *The Double Dealer* are worth further study. Congreve is an elegant, witty stylist and Hazlitt wrote of him, 'Every sentence is replete with sense and satire conveyed in the most polished and pointed terms.' *The Way Of The World* was a flop on its first appearance and Congreve was so dispirited by the experience that he vowed never to write for the theatre again.

For humanity and warmth there is nobody to match **GEORGE FARQUHAR** (1678-1707) who is responsible for two wonderful plays, *The Recruiting Officer* and *The Beaux' Strategem*. Both deal with imposture, in the first the plucky Silvia disguising herself as a man in order to test the truth of her soldier lover's affections. In *The Beaux' Strategem* our two heroes, Aimwell and Archer, begin by pretending to be something other than they are in order to pull off a nefarious plot. However, love, experience and common humanity win the day.

Other Restoration playwrights of note include SIR JOHN VANBRUGH (*The Provok'd Wife, The Relapse*) and SIR GEORGE ETHEREGE (*The Man of Mode*).

There was more serious drama as well. Beside Dryden's plays mention must be made of **THOMAS OTWAY**'s *Venice Preserved* (1682), the first great tragedy since Shakespeare. The eighteenth century was to see the rise of sentimental tragedy, which accompanied the rise of the middle classes, with few dramatists of great weight, though GEORGE LILLO's *The London Merchant* is of considerable interest.

Later in the eighteenth century, Goldsmith and **RICHARD BRINSLEY SHERIDAN** (1751-1816) wrote the most important plays of the period. Sheridan's *The School For Scandal* and *The Rivals* are gently satirical, witty comedies still popular today. Sheridan discarded the licentiousness of Restoration comedy but retained the wit.

THE AUGUSTAN AGE

The age of Dryden flows imperceptibly into the following Augustan Age (its idols Virgil, Ovid and Horace lived during the reign of the Roman emperor Augustus). This was particularly the period of Pope and Swift, but its limits are ill-defined, sometimes being pushed back as far as Dryden, so that the two periods may for practical purposes be regarded as one – when classicism reigned supreme. Its influence lasted until well into the eighteenth century.

ALEXANDER POPE (1688-1744) was as much pre-eminent in his own time as Dryden had been in his. He is often compared with Dryden for his clarity, directness and accuracy of writing. Read Pope's *Essay on Criticism, The Rape of the Lock* and the well-known *Essay on Man*. They are easy to read but difficult to imitate, the art that conceals art. Together with *The Dunciad* they make probably his most important work, although one could add his version of Homer's *Iliad*. The *Essay on Man* sets out a complete philosophy but lacks originality and inspiration, although it remains persuasive. Form was more important to Pope than content: he sought to achieve 'correctness of expression'. The Romantics of the next important period bitterly attacked him because he had become recognised as 'the supreme representative of the the classical school'. (John Mulan)

JONATHAN SWIFT (1667-1745), the brilliant satirist of *Gulliver's Travels,* also wrote *The Tale of the Tub* and *The Battle of the Books*, both highly amusing to read. The former is an uproarious allegorical satire on divisions in the Christian church, while the latter shows Swift as a supporter of the moderate Tories of the time. Satire is very difficult to write – it so easily becomes cynical or merely sarcastic. Swift superbly avoided both pitfalls. One of his most subtle and delicious pieces, *A Modest Proposal*, suggests that the economic problems of Ireland could be solved by eating Irish babies, and describes various appetising ways to serve them. *Gulliver's Travels* seems to have been relegated to the position of a childrens' classic. In its original form, it was highly unsuitable for children. Swift does not neglect the coarser problems of Gulliver's journeys in Lilliput and Brobdingnag, and the fourth book, set in the land of the Houhynhms, is a scabrous attack on contemporary morality. Among his many horrifying creations are the *strulbrugs*, who are immortal but still age at the normal rate, until they become so bitter, twisted and cynical that they are shunned by society.

RICHARD STEELE (1672-1729) and JOSEPH ADDISON (1672-1745), following Dryden and Pope, brought the essay to perfection as a literary form. In pure, elegant English, they commented on the manners and morals of the time, and greatly influenced the growing ideas of the middle class Christian citizen – respectable, dispassionate and tolerant. Most of their essays appeared in *The Tatler* (edited by Steele) and *The Spectator*. They are not without humour. Any anthology of English prose will contain essays by these two.

SAMUEL JOHNSON (1709-1784) is often regarded as the first great critic and was certainly a larger than life character. He succeeded Dryden and Pope as the premier man of letters of the eighteenth century. *The Vanity of Human Wishes* is arguably his best work. His *Lives of the English Poets* is interesting and opinionated, though Johnson is best known for the work of his biographer, **JAMES BOSWELL**, who should not only be read for his *Life of Johnson* but for the charming *Journal of a Tour to the Hebrides*.

The greatest prose writer of the latter part of this period was undoubtedly **DANIEL DEFOE** (1660-1731), who is generally regarded as the creator of the novel form. He is best remembered as the author of *Robinson Crusoe. Moll Flanders* is a major picaresque tale ('picaresque' from the Spanish *picaro* meaning 'rogue' – hence stories about rogues and vagabonds.) Defoe reveals a compelling documentary edge in *A Journal Of The Plague Year*. Ironically, the novel form emerged from a man to whom art and literary theory meant nothing, from a man who was not a gentleman but a tradesman dealing in commodities. Without benefit of a university education, Defoe was a man of wide learning and boundless curiosity. *Robinson Crusoe* began as an 'imaginary biography' of Alexander Selkirk, the noted castaway. In Defoe's hands it becomes not only a gripping story but an allegory of his own life, and an examination of the inescapable solitariness of each man in relation to God and himself.

For SAMUEL RICHARDSON (1680-1761) morality and religion are essential features. He was commissioned to compile a volume of *Familiar Letters* to serve as a model for the uneducated. Having embarked on this project, he soon began to see the narrative possibilities in the letter form and began the work which, as *Pamela, or Virtue Rewarded* (1750), is now regarded as the first true novel. It is now of more historic than artistic appeal. The suspense of the novel derives from whether or not Pamela Andrews will lose her virginity to the unscrupulous Mr B. *Clarissa* is driven by a similar plot device, and is brimful of almost sado-masochistic sexual tension.

LAURENCE STERNE (1713-1768) and TOBIAS SMOLLETT (1721-1771) are important to the development of the novel. Smollett's characters in such novels as *Roderick Random*, *Humphry Clinker* and *Peregrine Pickle* are grotesque and disgusting. He was a doctor and, it has been said, 'his works suggested the nightmare of an outraged hygienist.' The value of his work rests in brilliantly achieved episodes rather than cumulative effect. Sterne's extraordinary, discursive saga, *Tristram Shandy*, is famous for its many digressions, which are almost its *raison d'être*. It is almost a fore-runner of the stream of consciousness novels of the twentieth century.

The most important of the early novelists is **HENRY FIELDING** (1707-1754) whose twin masterpieces are *Tom*

Jones and *Joseph Andrews*. His sense of humour is rumbustious and slyly satirical, and his novels, though long, make an arresting antidote to the sententiousness of Richardson. Fielding was a man's man, and his female characters are a reflection of the way he viewed women. *Joseph Andrews* was first conceived as a satire on *Pamela*, dealing with Pamela's innocent brother, the eponymous Joseph, who is pursued by the sexually rapacious Lady Booby. In *Tom Jones*, the hero is himself a rascally but charming sexual predator, redeemed by his love for Sophia. The strength of the novel lies in its narrative drive and its evocatively drawn characters. Irony is implicit in everything Fielding wrote.

Mention must be made of the renowned Gothic writers of the later years of the eighteenth century. The horror tales of HORACE WALPOLE (*The Castle of Otranto*), MRS. RADCLIFFE (*The Mysteries of Udolpho*) and 'MONK' LEWIS (*Ambrosio, or the Monk*) are representative. They are called 'Gothic' from the revival of Gothic architecture at the time. They are amusing tales, not in the least terrifying, although meant to be so. 'Monk' Lewis is somewhat licentious and probably the most enjoyable.

The lesser poets of the eighteenth century divide roughly into two groups. Those in the first half of the century are often referred to as the Elegiac poets. Given the prevailing classicism of accepted verse forms, it is curious that these poets should be writing lyrical and musical verse, developing a new sensitivity to, and awareness of, Nature. This points towards the Romantic Revival which was to come at the end of the century. The move towards the Romantic age, however, was very gradual, as the classical forms were tenacious.

THOMAS GRAY (1715-1771) is probably the only poet of this period still popular today, and that only for his *Elegy, Written in a Country Churchyard*. This is simply written but strongly felt and effectively easy to speak. There are other poets worthy of note. EDWARD YOUNG (1683-1765) appealed to what seemed a growing taste for quiet melancholy reflection. *The Complaint* ('Night thoughts on Life, Death and Immortality') in nine parts, a series of somewhat sentimental meditations, became very popular. JAMES THOMPSON (1700-1748) was the first to use recognisably accurate observation of nature in *The Seasons* and *The Castle of Indolence*, a dream allegory in Spenserian stanzas. It is melodious and sometimes beautiful, although it never reaches the heights to which it aspires. These three poets represent the beginnings of the return to imagination in verse writing.

The poets of the second half of the century include **OLIVER GOLDSMITH** (1730-1774) with *The Travellers* and ***The Deserted Village***. Goldsmith's verse is still in classical rhyming couplets yet with a sympathetic quality uncommon to classicism. Goldsmith's reputation as a versatile and accomplished writer also rests on successful prose works, such as *The Vicar of Wakefield* and his celebrated comedy, ***She Stoops To Conquer*** which picks up the warm humanity of Farquhar's style with the plot developments of a Wycherley.

GEORGE CRABBE (1754-1832) differs strikingly from his fellow poets. The classical tradition still survives in his work but his tone is harsh, pessimistic and entirely unromantic. It is often referred to as 'unvarnished realism' and he was an expert in summarising a person or a place in a few lines. Horace Smith has called him "A Pope in worsted stockings." Crabbe is known today for *Peter Grimes*, set into operatic form by Benjamin Britten in the twentieth century but much more effective as a poem. It is a superb piece of writing. Crabbe became well-known following *The Village* (1783) which shows unyielding, remorseless realism in his description of every existence. Not by any means a romantic, he was nevertheless interested in ordinary, humble people.

WILLIAM COWPER (1731-1800) is best known for the comic ballad *John Gilpin* and *The Task*, equally as good. *The Castaway*, a short poem intended lyrically but reflecting an anguished mind, seems strange to us, the form and vocabulary over-elaborate, perhaps signalling the need for a new way of writing.

ROBERT BURNS (1759-1796), the supreme poet of Scotland, represents a complete break with classicism. He was a farmer, from a family of poor farmers, living in Ayrshire. *Tam O'Shanter* is a glorious example of his writing and there is a host of love and war poems. His feeling for the Scottish countryside is passionately evoked, and there is plenty of earthy humour.

WILLIAM BLAKE is a very important literary figure, though his work stands outside all movements. Highly original, painter as well as poet, Blake had a mystical strain delighting in allegory. *Songs of Innocence* and *Songs of Experience* are essential reading. *Tyger, Tyger* and *Jerusalem* are probably his best known works. He is remembered, too, for his prophetic writings, *The Book of Thel* and *The Marriage of Heaven and Hell*. Blake had no formal education and his early work was revolutionary and often satirical in tone. The gloom, mysticism and remarkable imagery of his later work conveyed a powerful sense of evil, and forgiveness was to emerge as a major theme.

THE ROMANTIC REVIVAL

THE ROMANTICS

The early nineteenth century saw a determined rejection of conservative classical writing. In its place was substituted a new imaginative creativity. Classicism had become over-formal, stressing the impersonal aspects of life. The new romanticism concerned itself with the natural, the 'ordinary' individual, imagination and sensibility – the essence of individuality. Whilst classicists wrote objectively of things outside themselves, romantics were involved subjectively with thought and feeling. It might best be described as a swing from extraversion to introversion. The change was already spasmodically apparent during the eighteenth century, but there was no great writer to take hold of it to fashion something new from it. The twin assault on contemporary sensibilities launched by **WILLIAM WORDSWORTH** (1770-1850) and **SAMUEL TAYLOR COLERIDGE** (1772-1834) was to change the tone of literature irredeemably. The 'revival' looked back to the Elizabethans and, more importantly, even further back to the age of the ballads. Ballads had been composed for ordinary people, expressing ordinary thought and feeling and situation, to which the new romanticism added the moral influence of Nature upon man.

1798, which saw the publication of *Lyrical Ballads* by Wordsworth and Coleridge, is the date generally considered to mark the the beginning of the Romantic Revival. This is, perhaps, unfortunate, for Coleridge had already achieved a reputation as a poet by 1796 with *Poems on Various Subjects* (running to three editions) and Wordsworth was writing as early as 1793, his *An Evening's Walk* showing an awareness of aspects of Nature hitherto unnoticed by other poets. ROBERT SOUTHEY (1774-1843), a friend of both Wordsworth and Coleridge, is the third of the so-called Lake Poets, 'the first generation of romantics.'

American Independence, the French Revolution, and the accelerating industrial revolution were the social and political movements of the time, giving rise to a general yearning for greater freedom. The Romantic Revival was a very real change of direction. For the first time in many years poetry became more dominant in English literature than prose.

There is no doubt that Wordsworth is one of the greatest of English writers and is, at his best, unmatched. Though he achieved social status, becoming Poet Laureate, his later work is greatly inferior to the work composed before 1810, upon which his reputation is based. His influence was so powerful that it stretches right up to the present day. He, Coleridge and Southey contended that the poet should 'choose incidents and situations from common life' and 'throw over them a certain colouring of imagination, whereby ordinary things should be presented to the mind in an unusual aspect' tracing 'the primary laws of our nature'. The quotations come from the famous *Preface to Lyrical Ballads* which is another of the key works on the art of poetry, to be compared with Sidney and Dryden, and which contains the famous definition of poetry as 'emotion recollected in tranquillity.'

Wordsworth is the Nature poet par excellence, practically everything he wrote deriving from his sense of the closeness of nature to mankind:

> For I have learned
> To look on Nature, not as in the hour
> Of thoughtless youth, but hearing oftentimes
> The still, sad music of humanity,
> Not harsh, nor grating yet of ample power
> To chasten and subdue. And I have felt
> A presence that disturbs me with the joy
> Of elevated thoughts, a sense sublime
> Of something far more deeply interfused,
> Whose dwelling is the light of setting sun,
> And the round ocean, and the living air,
> And the blue sky, and in the mind of man...

Wordsworth's apparent simplicity is deceptive. He is a careful writer, exact in his use of rhythm and scansion, and knows exactly when to break a rhythm. His short poems present little difficulty of comprehension, though for speaking aloud the punctuation should be carefully followed. He achieved his effects in a manner of which one is aware but unable to fasten upon, save as a kind of mysticism in touch with Nature and Reality. Of his remarkably consistent early output you should read *The Solitary Reaper*, a perfectly constructed poem, as well as *Lines Written in Early Spring, Resolution and Independence, Ode to Duty* and the *Lucy* poems. His *I wandered lonely as a cloud* might well be compared with Herrick's *Daffodils*.

Wordsworth's better sonnets are as distinctive as those of Shakespeare and Milton – try *Lines Written Upon Westminster Bridge* and *The World Is Too Much With Us*. His longer poems retain the simplicity he desired, although occasionally he is inattentive to the 'language of ordinary man.' *Michael* expounds his belief that work is the antidote to all vexations: a poem deeply felt, with moving verse paragraphs near the end. (A 'verse paragraph' is simply a section of a long poem which has been divided into paragraphs of irregular numbers of lines.) He seeks to create atmosphere, mood and the emotions of his people without ever describing them directly.

Ode: Intimations of Immortality and *Tintern Abbey* are arguably his twin masterpieces. His uncompleted epic, *The Prelude,* seeks to show the growth of a poet's mind and soul using his own life as subject. Try the first two books, and book five, for there are magnificent passages to be found, especially his experiences as a young boy.

Wordsworth has been accused of lacking a sense of humour. This is certainly true of his later work but look at *Expostulation and Reply* before concurring.

Samuel Taylor Coleridge is less consistent than Wordsworth, but a handful of his best poems rank with the finest in the language. He was a strange, dour man. His part in *Lyrical Ballads* was to write of the supernatural in such a way as to make it seem natural. Apart from Shakespeare there are now probably more books, essays and critiques written on him than on any other poet. His life and works seem to have a peculiar fascination for the twentieth century.

His masterpieces are **The Rime of the Ancient Mariner**, a bizarre and gothic tale of suffering and redemption in ballad form; **Christabel**, another incomplete epic on an horrific subject; and **Kubla Khan**, a short poem which he claimed to have written straight off after having a most vivid dream. He further stated that the poem owes its brevity to his being interrupted by 'a man from Porlock.' He constantly tinkered with all three of these poems. Certainly nothing similar has ever been written by anyone else. Perfectly conceived, they are instances of an intellectual-intuitional split in consciousness. They are also perfect examples of poems having layers of meaning.

Whilst these three poems are extraordinary, there are others equally beautiful. **Frost at Midnight** and **Dejection: An Ode** should be read. *France – An Ode* and *Fears in Solitude* are worth looking at. His 'literary biography,' called, logically enough, *Biographia Literaria* is the product of a highly developed and original brain, although he has been charged with deliberate plagiarism. His sections on Shakespeare are among the best about that dramatist. *Biographia Literaria* contains a sentence which encapsulates Coleridge's tone: "If a man could walk through Paradise in a dream, and have a flower presented to him as a pledge that his soul had really been there, and if he found that flower in his hand when he awoke – Aye! and what then?"

Southey is not in the same league as Wordsworth and Coleridge. *The Inchcape Rock* and *The Battle of Blenheim* are worth reading, as are his *Lives of Wesley* and *Nelson*.

Wordsworth, Coleridge and Southey were the first generation of Romantics. They did not admire, or indeed approve of, the second generation.

GEORGE GORDON, LORD BYRON (1788-1824) leapt to fame with the publication in 1812 of *Childe Harold's*

Pilgrimage. ('Childe' has the old English meaning of 'knight' and 'Harold' is a thinly-disguised Byron himself.) The failure of the French Revolution and the disillusion which followed all over Europe created a mood admirably suited to the times. Sometimes sentimental, often cynical passages describe 'Harold's' travels across Europe and the East, during which he becomes disillusioned and seeks to escape reality. Byron had a powerful style which often communicates with the reader or listener, and if passages are carefully selected he is fascinating to read. The poem is divided into cantos ('canto' means a grouping of stanzas into blocks, divisions of a work.) ***Converse with Nature*** (C.3 ST. 23-26 and 37), ***Once More Upon the Waters*** (C.3 St.1-4), ***Body and Soul*** (C.3 St.2-5) should certainly be read and *Byron's Hopes* (C.4 St.8-10) might be considered. Read also his poems *The Prisoner of Chillon* (including the opening sonnet), ***So We'll Go No More A'Roving, She Walks in Beauty*** and some of *Don Juan.* Byron's masterpiece was ***The Vision of Judgement***, an hilarious satire on Southey's poem of the same title. Southey had attacked Byron for 'Those monstrous combinations of horrors and mockery, lewdness and impiety' in his poem about George III rising from his grave, discomfiting the Devil, and, following a testimonial from Washington, finally being received into Heaven. Byron lampoons Southey derisively and treats the late king's appearance before the Heavenly tribunal with mockery. It landed Byron's publisher with a heavy fine for treating King George disrespectfully. Both poems are well worth reading.

PERCY BYSSHE SHELLEY (1792-1822), rebel, idealist and lover of liberty, was the opposite of the cynical Byron, hence their attraction to each other. Shelley rejected established religion, called himself an atheist, but was, in fact a pantheist 'inspired by love; a love not limited to men and women but extending to every living creature, to flowers and to the elements, to the whole of Nature.' (John Mulgan) Thus his lyrics have a certain freshness, recalling the free air, the clouds and the sky. Read ***The Skylark, Ode to the West Wind,***

The Cloud, and feel the sense of freedom they create. Try to read the whole of *Adonais* with its varying tones – 'solemn music' on the death of Keats. Read **Ozymandias**, the sonnet *England in 1819* and **Stanzas Written in Dejection Near Naples**, which is superbly constructed. *The Masque of Anarchy* and *The Aziola* are also worth attention. Shelley wrote an essay, **A Defence of Poetry** , which is worth comparing with those of Sidney and Dryden. In this work Shelley argued that the poets are the 'founders of civil society' and that 'poets are the unacknowledge legislators of the world.' He also said that 'The secret of morals is love; or a giving out of our own nature, and an identification of ourselves with the beautiful.'

JOHN KEATS (1792-1821) wrote slow, rich verse, beautiful and perfectly constructed. He was a 'poet's poet'. There is no lesson to be taught in Keats save that 'Beauty is Truth, Truth Beauty.' Read the odes, **On a Grecian Urn, The Nightingale**, *To Melancholy, To Autumn* and, as a contrast, **La Belle Dame Sans Merci**, a ballad. **The Eve of St. Agnes** celebrates a well-known myth, and the sonnets *When I have Fears* and *The Human Seasons* are finely written. You will either love Keats or find him tedious. His longer works, *Endymion* and *Lamia* have some good passages but lack form. **Isabella, or the Pot of Basil** is an evocative tale, based on a story from Boccaccio's *Decameron*, possibly his masterpiece.

Other good poets of this generation were THOMAS MOORE (1779-1852 – *Irish Melodies, Loves of the Angels*), WALTER SAVAGE LANDOR (1775-1864 – *Pericles and Aspasia, Dirce*), LEIGH HUNT (1784-1859 – *The Story of Rimini, Jenny Kissed Me*) and THOMAS HOOD (1799-1845 – *Song of the Shirt, The Bridge of Sighs*), who are worth reading but more or less forgotten today.

In prose, CHARLES LAMB (1775-1834) is notable for his writing, especially on poets contemporary with Shakespeare and his *Essays of Elia*. His friend WILLIAM HAZLITT (1778-1830) was an outstanding critic, perceptive and lively and THOMAS DE QUINCY (1785-1859) is known for his *Confessions of an English Opium-Eater* and *Reminiscences of the*

English Lake Poets. Perhaps his two most popular essays are the humorous *On Murder as One of the Fine Arts* (recommended to potential homicides) and *On the Knocking at the Gate in Macbeth,* the only element of grotesque comedy in the play. If you can find it, read *Suspiria de profundis* for its unusual use of vowel sounds, what T. H. Williams called 'vowel-music'.

THE VICTORIAN POETS

The Victorian Poets differ from the Romantics in their attitudes. Their work was a reaction to the excesses of Romanticism rather than a sharp change of direction. 1832 is often quoted as the beginning of the Victorian Period (though Victoria did not ascend the throne until 1837). By this date, Shelley, Keats and Byron were dead, Coleridge was dying and Wordsworth long finished as a great poet and was now a confirmed conservative. That year saw the Reform Bill in Parliament, giving the middle-class the vote and gradually making the industrialist dominant over the landowner in the economy.

The main feature of the period was the obvious supremacy of prose over verse, and the enormous increase in popularity of the novel. The industrial revolution was in full flood, economic prosperity was available at home for the entrepreneur, Imperial glory shone abroad – the times should have been peaceful and happy. But Darwin's *Origin of Species* wracked society with religious controversy, and the Irish Famines, Chartist Riots, dreadful factory conditions, agitation for trades unions rights and the moral struggle between money and common decency all militated against quietness and peace.

When a society is threatened with disintegration, the only refuge seems to be to try to impose submission to orthodox traditions; there was an excessive fear of too much change during these years. Rejection of Romantic extravagances did not prove difficult but the Romantic influence was not defeated and continued into the twentieth century. This period may be said to have continued until the world war in 1914, although there is often reference to EDWARDIAN and GEORGIAN periods after 1900.

The period had a substantial number of interesting poets. **ALFRED LORD TENNYSON** (1809-1892), greatly read by our grandfathers, **ROBERT BROWNING** (1812-1899) and the PRE-RAPHAELITE BROTHERHOOD should be investigated.

Tennyson and Browning, taken together, provide a clear contrast, and embody both the vices and virtues of the styles of the age. Tennyson was popular, technically a master, skilful and melodious. Humbert Wolfe has referred to 'Tennyson's honey'. Try *In Memoriam* quietly reflecting on immortality on the death of a friend, often beautiful in some of its four-line stanzas, which shows both Tennyson's strengths and weaknesses, *Morte D'Arthur* is part of a long Arthurian verse epic, *Idylls of the King* and is wonderfully sonorous when spoken aloud. *The Lotus Eaters* is an enchanting poem, and other major short works are *The Poet's Song, The Lady of Shalott* and *Break, Break*. Tennyson was jealous of form in a poem.

Browning is virtually the reverse of Tennyson, lyrical certainly, but less interested in the music of words than in the study of human nature and the inherent drama of relationships. The well-known words from *Pippa Passes* beginning 'The year's at the spring' show him, perhaps, too easily optimistic. Try *Home Thoughts from Abroad, Home Thoughts from the Sea, Prospice, The Lost Mistress. Rabbi Ben Ezra, How They Brought The Good News from Ghent to Aix, My Last Duchess* and of course *The Pied Piper* are excellent pieces for speaking aloud.

Browning's wife, ELIZABETH BARRETT-BROWNING, is now perhaps best known for her dramatic elopement with Browning from her tyrannical father. She was an interesting, if sometimes turgid, poet in her own right and her best short pieces, the sonnets *How Do I Love Thee?* and *Remember Me* are exquisite.

The third major poet of the Victorian age was
MATTHEW ARNOLD (1822-1888), son of the famous
headmaster of Rugby, Dr Arnold. He was to develop into a
famous and authoritative figure, and both his prose and
poetry can sometimes be a little pompous. During his
lifetime he made great efforts to improve the standards of
education and was, for much of his life, a professor at Oxford.
His most perfect short poem is *On Dover Beach*, while his
most famous pieces are probably *Sohrab and Rustum* (which
has passages of incandescent grandeur) and *The Scholar
Gipsy*.

Victorian poets well worth looking at include the famous
dialect poet WILLIAM BARNES (1801-86 – *Poems of Rural
Life*) and the marvellously iconoclastic and cynical
ARTHUR HUGH CLOUGH (1819-61 – *The Bothie of
Tober-na-Vuolich, The Latest Decalogue* and *Amours De Voyage*).
COVENTRY PATMORE (1823-96) is a lyric poet of great
sensitivity. Try his *Faithful For Ever* and *Magna Est Veritas*
which can be found in many anthologies. Anthologies will
also give you a taste of other, less famous, Victorian poets
such as WILLIAM THOM, THOMAS BABINGTON
MACAULAY (known for his *Lays of Ancient Rome*),
THOMAS LOVELL BEDDOES, EDWARD FITZGERALD
(whose translation of *The Rubaiyat of Omar Khayyam* has
never been surpassed), GEORGE MEREDITH and
WILLIAM ALLINGHAM.

Several writers best known as novelists were also
considerable poets. CHARLES KINGSLEY (*The Water
Babies*) wrote some fine lyrics and both **EMILY BRONTE**
and, late in the century, **THOMAS HARDY** (see below)
were poets of the first rank. Emily Bronte's *Cold In The Earth*
and *Last Lines* are magnificent, passionate pieces in the same
spirit as her novels. Hardy's reputation as a poet has, in the
latter part of the twentieth century, eclipsed his reputation as
a novelist. A lyrical poet at once tender-hearted and sensitive
with an ironic, satirical strain breaking through at times, he
believed (in his poetry) that Nature reveals 'a conscious

purpose.' He had a strong sense of the adversities Fate places before us and was only too conscious of the forces, both from within and without, that militate against a pleasant and successful life! There are many short poems of great sensitivity which can be explored, notably *At The Railway Station, Upway, The Parasol, She, To Him, In Time of The Breaking of Nations, The Darkling Thrush,* I Need Not Go, Afterwards, Regret Not Me. and *Snow In The Suburbs*.

The most important of the self-styled Pre-Raphaelite poets were DANTE GABRIEL ROSSETTI (1828-1882) and his sister, **CHRISTINA ROSSETTI** (1830-1894). There were painters as well as poets in the Pre-Raphaelite Brotherhood (Millais, Holman Hunt and Burne-Jones among them), all reacting against the conventional and looking back to Medievalism (literally 'pre-Raphael, the great Renaissance painter). They formulated the doctrine of 'Art for Art's Sake', making Keats their ideal poet. Their work appears in many anthologies and should be glanced at. They might be thought too sentimental but there are those who consider them superb.

Of Dante Gabriel Rossetti try *The Blessed Damozel, Eden Bower* and a sequence of sonnets called *The House of Life*. Christina is best remembered for her evocative *Goblin Market* and the collection of sonnets called *Monna Innominata*

ALGERNON CHARLES SWINBURNE (1837-1909) ought to be noted. At first a Pre-Raphaelite, his other discipline was music rather than painting. His work is sonorous, using both vowels and consonants in groups to enrich his verse. His imagery seems weak but there are subtle nuances of harmony and rhythm in the sounds of his writing, which perhaps reflects his interest in music. *Poems and Ballads* challenged the morality of the Victorian period, outraged the orthodox but pleased the young for his rejection of convention and his stress on sensuality. *Songs Before Sunrise* could well be read, as could *Tristram in Lyonesse*, generally thought to be his best work. He was a critic as well and, like Lamb before him, campaigned on behalf of Shakespeare's contemporaries in *Essays and Studies*, a valuable source of information and opinion.

GERARD MANLEY HOPKINS (1844-1889) is a Victorian in time but his work is a forerunner of the twentieth century. A convert to the Jesuits, he was refused permission to publish any poems. None of his work appeared until 1918, nearly thirty years after his death. Hopkins reacted against the general Victorian vogue for tunefulness and was highly original in his approach. A master of complex sentences, alliteration and sprung rhythm – the jumping of the voice from stress to stress with varied numbers of unstressed syllables between. This he called, 'scanning by accents and stresses alone'. He took delight in the use of hard consonants to give his poems emotional power, and he considerably influenced twentieth century verse writing. Look at *The Wreck of the Deutschland, Pied Beauty, Hurrahing in Harvest, No worst, there is none, Inversnaid*, some of *Sibyl's Leaves* and, clearly illustrative of his use of alliteration, *The Sea and the Skylark*. Hopkins was always concerned with the transience of beauty compared with the permanence of God.

THE NINETEENTH CENTURY NOVEL

The novel is the dominant form of the nineteenth century in the same way that drama dominates the early seventeenth century. During the course of the century, it developed from the rambling, picaresque and often licentious tales common to Fielding and Smollet to become a highly disciplined, structured form of considerable philosophical weight. Interestingly, this was not a development in English literature alone. Among others the century saw, in France, Zola, Flaubert and Balzac; in Russia, Turgenev, Tolstoy and Dostoyevsky.

In England, SIR WALTER SCOTT (1771-1832) was an important, prolific and popular writer of historical romances. His work is long and difficult to read but *The Talisman* is short and interesting, especially for Scott's attitude to his hero and the romanticising of Saladin, the Kurdish leader opposed to Richard Coeur-de-Lion during the Crusades. Scott depicts Saladin as a chivalrous, loyal and magnanimous Muslim, even curing Richard of an illness, a reputation that has lasted to the present day. Scott's best known works are *Ivanhoe* and *Kenilworth*, at least one of which should be read. His collected works are known as *The Waverley Novels*.

JANE AUSTEN (1775-1817) is one of the three or four greatest English writers, with a remarkable grasp of character and form. ***Mansfield Park*** is often held to be her best novel, although ***Emma*** is a close contender for this accolade. ***Pride and Prejudice*** and ***Sense and Sensibility*** are her most popular books. Her last novel, *Persuasion* is rather different in tone and style, with an air of melancholy missing in her early novels. Jane Austen wrote in a subtle, ironic style, often missed by the casual reader, and there is a humorous tolerance towards her characters. Throughout her work there is a sense of moral rectitude, never specifically stated, but which must become part of a character before that character may be permitted to reach a happy conclusion. Both Elizabeth and Darcy must surrender their pride and their prejudice before they may be happily married, for instance. There is a brilliant command of language, with well nigh perfect syntax. Sentences are often long with many subordinate clauses and phrases, but the parts are perfectly balanced. Austen is a quiet writer whose world encompasses a narrow scope, but it is exquisitely drawn. She gradually gains one's admiration when one realises that she is gently mocking the reader as well as her characters.

A curious feature of her novels is that although living during the greatest upheaval in European history – the aftermath of the French Revolution and the Napoleonic wars – there is never any reference to it, only occasionally a character appearing in military uniform.

MRS GASKELL (1810-1865) is famous for *Cranford*, an amusing portrait of a Cheshire village based on her native Knutsford. Like Austen, her scope is small and the writing fine, but it produces a gentle, amusing and civilised novel. Her other works include *Mary Barton, Wives and Daughters* and a remarkable *Life of Charlotte Brontë*, which is interesting background to understanding the novels of the Brontë sisters.

There were four Brontë children – the three female novelists, **CHARLOTTE BRONTË** (1816-55), **EMILY BRONTË** (1818-48) and **ANNE BRONTË** (1820-49) and their disreputable painter brother, Branwell. Their characters and situation have attracted as much attention as their literary output and are, in a sense, as remarkable. Crammed together in a tiny parsonage in Haworth on the edge of the Yorkshire moors, they lived with a stern Irish father in genteel poverty. Their only escape was into their imaginations, and the landscape of Yorkshire informs everything they wrote.

The eldest sister, Charlotte, is the most accomplished of the three. Her masterpiece is undoubtedly *Jane Eyre*, the classic romance between a plain governess and her difficult, masterful employer, Edward Rochester. The novel has Gothic elements and there is an element of sado-masochism in Jane's passions, which all help to give the driving narrative and complex language their unique flavour. A similar sense of repressed sexual hysteria informs her other major novel, *Villette*, another story of a governess, this time set in Belgium. *Shirley* and *The Professor* are her other works. Charlotte was the only one of the sisters to marry, late in life.

Emily Brontë's only novel is **Wuthering Heights** but this, in itself, has assured her of a place in any literary history. It is an extraordinary story of wild passion on the moors, though the famous story of Heathcliff and Catherine Earnshaw only occupies the first half of the story, the resolution of the passions and problems being the responsibility of their children. The novel is oddly and unsatisfactorily structured but the language and the characters highly memorable.

Anne is remembered for *The Tenant of Wildfell Hall* and *Agnes Grey,* but she only intermittently achieves the power of her sisters. Their brother Branwell drank himself to death.

An interesting footnote is that the work of the three sisters was published under male pseudonyms – respectively, Currer, Ellis and Acton Bell – because it was felt that their books would not be accepted by contemporary society if issued under female names. Women writers of the day were expected only to write about romance and polite society. The Brontës' work is never polite.

WILLIAM MAKEPEACE THACKERAY (1811-63) is an amusing and prolific writer, best known for **Vanity Fair** in which he created the (in)famous Becky Sharpe, a wilful woman of great personal charm. It is one of the half dozen most popular nineteenth century novels, witty, amusing and sometimes acerbic. His other work is less highly regarded but is of some interest, including *Barry Lyndon, The Rose and the Ring* and *The Virginians.* Thackeray has a tendency to address the reader directly, reminiscent of Fielding and Smollett, of whom he is the spiritual heir.

The next major novelist, and probably the most famous of all nineteenth century novelists, is **CHARLES DICKENS** (1812-1870). Full of humanity and wit, and brightly written, his books reflect the social conditions of the times. Many of his novels were originally written for magazines, one instalment per month, so his composition is often erratic. He sometimes falls prey to the sentimental and melodramatic and his characters are often wonderfully odd. He is perhaps too much the journalist and not enough the artist; but he could write superbly, especially in his many descriptive passages. His sentences are often long, with many qualifying clauses and phrases, but he is highly speakable. His best books are tremendously exciting, intricately plotted and with considerable moral weight and anger at the injustices of the age. The towering peaks of his achievement are *Bleak House* (with its blistering attack on British law), *Great Expectations* (perhaps his most perfectly-constructed book) and *Little Dorrit*, though the angelic heroine is, today, a little hard to take. His innocent female characters are thinly drawn, his greatest weakness as a writer. As well as the three masterpieces, you should try one or more of the popular classics - *Oliver Twist, David Copperfield, A Christmas Carol, Nicholas Nickleby, The Pickwick Papers, A Tale of Two Cities* and *Hard Times*. Dickens gave the world many characters which have become part of the popular imagination – Scrooge, Fagin, Squeers, Miss Havisham and Uriah Heap among them.

Compare Dickens with **ANTHONY TROLLOPE** (1815-1870), a more moderate writer with characters drawn from real life, who writes at a leisurely pace on middle-class provincial life. His *Barchester* novels are deservedly regarded as very good literature, calm, shrewd, the characters well drawn and the stories effectively told. Try *The Warden* or *Barchester Towers*. Trollope went on to write another series of novels collectively known as *The Pallisers*. His finest achievement, and a novel which stands quite alone, is *The Way We Live Now* which is extraordinarily modern in tone.

GEORGE ELIOT (1819-80) was, in reality, another woman writer, Mary Ann Evans. She was freed from her rather narrow religious views by a Coventry manufacturer, and was later notorious for living with, but not marrying, a free-thinking Canon. She is one of the great serious novelists and her style, while occasionally leaden, manages to tackle weighty matters with grace, style and humour. Her masterpiece, a panoramic saga of contemporary life, is *Middlemarch*, which tells of Dorothea Brooke, her middle aged suitor Mr Casaubon (who might be a blood relative of Mr Knightly in *Emma*) and her fatal passion for the feckless Will Ladislaw. *The Mill on the Floss* is a marvellous tale of a family growing up in rural surroundings and has an exciting climax during a flood. If these two appeal, explore her further with the relatively short *Silas Marner*, the impressive *Daniel Deronda,* and, a tale of rustic passion, *Adam Bede.*

WILKIE COLLINS (1824-89) was a friend of Dickens and is often credited with inventing the detective novel with *The Moonstone*, in which Sergeant Cuff solves the complicated mystery of a stolen yellow diamond. Collins was extraordinarily prolific, strongly plot-driven and often absurdly melodramatic. Apart from *The Moonstone*, his major work is *The Woman In White*, a powerful psychological thriller.

Before we come to Hardy, the latest of the great nineteenth century novelists, there are other writers worth mentioning and some of whose work is very readable. Roughly in date order, the following seems a fair selection – FREDERICK MARRYAT (*Mr Midshipman Easy*), CHARLES READE (*The Cloister and the Hearth*), GEORGE MEREDITH (*The Egoist* and *Diana of the Crossways*) and SAMUEL BUTLER (*Erewhon* and *The Way of All Flesh*).

There was a group known as the Aesthetic School. WALTER PATER and **OSCAR WILDE** (see page 69) are the best known. They rejected the Victorian idea that 'the beautiful' is necessarily 'the good', and that perfect morality is the basis of good art. Nothing is necessary for good art, they asserted, except art itself. Wilde's only novel *The Picture of*

Dorian Gray is a flawed but fascinating achievement, while his short stories for children (*The Happy Prince, The House of Pomegranates, The Selfish Giant* etc) are beautifully conceived and constructed.

THOMAS HARDY (1840-1928) is an important and still controversial writer, admired these days as much for his poetry as for his many novels, all of which were written before the turn of the century. *Tess of the D'Urbervilles* and *Jude The Obscure* are his masterpieces, both of which involved him in scandal and public outrage as he refused to accept the validity of contemporary morality. Tess Durbeyfield, seduced by the wicked Alec D'Urbeville, is seen not as the conventional 'fallen woman' but as a tragic victim of social and religious prejudice. In *Jude*, the character of Susanna reads like someone created after Freud's discoveries about the human psyche, but in fact predates the influential psychoanalyst by a couple of decades. *The Return of the Native, The Mayor of Casterbridge* and *Far From the Madding Crowd* are the other major novels, for Hardy was prolific and variable. His mood is often tragic, even pessimistic – Nature and Destiny combine to frustrate the best efforts of human beings and exert a malevolent influence on them. This is leavened by some humour, mostly from his rustic characters.

His influence lived on into the twentieth century, after the critical roasting given to *Jude* caused him to give up prose writing. D. H. Lawrence could not have written as he did without Hardy's pioneering work before him, and MARY WEBB (1881-1927), a Shropshire writer, has a similar feel in her romantic, earthy novels *Precious Bane, The Golden Arrow* and *Gone To Earth*.

Though the work of American writers is outside the scope of this guide, there are some key figures whose influence on English literature has been so pervasive that they cannot be ignored. One such is **HENRY JAMES** (1843-1916), who has been described as a decadent Jane Austen. The precision of his style is certainly comparable but his subject matter is far broader and his tone more cynical. James settled in Europe in 1875 and his influences are more European than most other American writers of the period. Indeed, from 1898, he lived in Sussex. His most popular novels and short stories (a form in which he was a master) deal with the effect of the older civilisation of Europe on American life – *Daisy Miller, The Europeans* and the exquisite ***Portrait of a Lady***. His most famous works are ***The Turn Of The Screw***, a classic ghost story, and ***Washington Square***, about a plain heiress and her acutely intelligent father who can neither ignore or forgive his daughter's failings. His last three great novels are *The Wings of the Dove, The Ambassadors* and *The Golden Bowl.*

On the cusp of the twentieth century, **JOSEPH CONRAD** (1857-1924) was of Polish origin and learned English quite late in life. His English is therefore almost too precise, though with idiosyncratic sentence structure. He became a master of rich, sensuous expression, much concerned with the mystery of life, and considerably obsessed with the unknown - a constant theme being spiritual breakdown. Most of his novels are about the sea. *Lord Jim* is well-known, *Typhoon* a large important work and *The Secret Agent* uncommonly effective. His finest works are probably **Heart of Darkness** and **Nostromo**. Conrad, like Hardy, is pessimistic and his prose so dense that it may take a while to enjoy. It is, however, worth persisting, for there are passages of power and great beauty. Hardy, Conrad and the poetry of the young Eliot institute the sense of disaster, disillusion and faithlessness endemic to twentieth century writing.

DRAMA 1800 - 1914

The distinguishing characteristic of the nineteenth and early twentieth centuries is the revival and development of the drama. The nineteenth century provided the theatres, the twentieth the drama. Until the last quarter of the nineteenth century there was little drama that has survived, but the writers of that final period established the bedrock on which modern drama has built so prolifically.

In the early 1800s, the Industrial Revolution drove people from the countryside into the towns in search of work. The social history of this period shows the appalling conditions of work in factories and life at home, for those who could find a home, was little better. Living became arduous, dreary and expensive. There arose a strong demand for simple escapist entertainment, a yearning for fantasy. The romance absent from real life, song, colour, magic and spectacle could offer at least a temporary escape from a grim existence. Theatre was ready to supply this need. Between 1800 and 1840 some twenty 'minor' theatres were built and the use of increasingly sophisticated stage machinery created spectacular effects. It was the age of the grand actor and the grand spectacle, with trains rushing across the stage, magnificent scenes below the sea, and simplistic melodrama (literally, drama with incidental music). Minor theatres were not licensed to present plays, as such, but managers got around this by adding music to the drama.

David Garrick's new lighting system and the final banishment of the downstage doors in 1822, saw the picture-frame stage finally established. The later introduction of gas lighting and limelight enabled the auditorium to be completely darkened and some makeshift control of light on the stage (the first dimmers!) completed the change.

Only three London theatres were permitted entirely spoken drama, but a movement for 'Freedom of the Theatre' developed, to present spoken drama as well as spectacle in the minor theatres. In 1843 the licences were revoked, allowing all theatres to present any kind of production. From 1865 to 1900, another twenty or so theatres were built in London and in the first decade of the twentieth century yet another dozen: thus theatrical entertainment of some kind became generally popular amongst all classes of people. Plays were written for these theatres, of course, but their authors had little dramatic skill, nor was it demanded of them. Bernard Brixey's *The Kingdom of Transpontus* (now out of print, but available through some libraries) traces some of these popular entertainments. Examples include *Black-Eyed Susan, The Murder at Midnight, Alone in the Pirate's Lair, The Triumph of Neptune* and *The Female Sailor,* none of which has survived except in the Penny-Plain-Twopence-Coloured toy theatres that were the vogue at the end of the century and still survive amongst collectors. Classical revivals continued with Restoration plays and Shakespeare adapted for the great actor-managers of the times. Many plays were altered to allow for spectacular settings, often architecturally accurate reproductions of, say, the Roman Senate in *Julius Caesar* or the centre of Verona for *Romeo and Juliet.*

The greatest actor-knight of the century was Sir Henry Irving who, with Ellen Terry, ruled the West End from the Lyceum Theatre. A little later, Sir Herbert Beerbohm Tree's spectacular productions at Her Majesty's Theatre included *A Midsummer Night's Dream* with live rabbits and butterflies used to create the impression of the magic wood.

The first important fore-runner of modern drama was T.S. (TOM) ROBERTSON (1838-1871). He was an actor, producer, playwright, songwriter and scene-painter and was one of a large family of actors (including Madge Kendal). In 1864 he presented two of his own plays, *David Garrick* and *Society,* which for the first time demanded a degree of naturalism in design and acting. Robertson provided extensive stage directions for the actors and his characters were recognisably human, speaking natural everyday Victorian language. A series of plays followed, all with monosyllabic titles, of which the only one remembered and occasionally revived is *Caste* (1867). Robertson, by modern standards, was not a good playwright but to him goes the credit for the introduction of the play form we are familiar with today.

DION BOUCICAULT (1820-90) was a prolific Irish writer, responsible for several effective melodramas (such as *The Shaughraun*) and adaptations of popular novels (*The Corsican Brothers*). His best play, still revived today, is the comedy, *London Assurance*, which is reminiscent of the later Restoration playwrights and memorable for the character of Sir Harcourt Courtly.

From 1890 onwards there developed a conflict between what may be called the commercial theatre and the theatre of ideas. In fact, neither could remain uninfluenced by the other, and both popular, escapist entertainment and symbolic drama attained a new seriousness and theatricality, respectively, as the century wore on.

Strictly speaking, the fathers of modern drama, **HENRIK IBSEN** (1828-1906), **AUGUST STRINDBERG** (1849-1912) and **ANTON CHEKHOV** (1860-1904) are outside the scope of this guide, being Norwegian, Swedish and Russian, respectively. However, their influence on playwriting is so vast that they must be discussed in at least some detail.

HENRIK IBSEN revolutionised not only the form of drama – apparently naturalistic but with strong symbolic elements – but the content. He was a controversial figure both during his lifetime and for many years afterwards. Ibsen not only refused to accept conventional morality, but challenged it head on. He dramatised the psyches of his characters and was one of the founding fathers of Naturalism. After a number of largely forgotten verse dramas dealing with the mythology and history of his homeland, he produced two verse masterpieces, *Peer Gynt* and *Brand*, which were virtually unstageable in contemporary terms but which have been successfully staged with today's more fluid conventions. After this, he began to write about his own society, though, as he exiled himself to Italy, distance lent objectivity if not warmth to his work. Many of his greatest plays are set in homes which have become prisons, against which the individual must struggle to achieve any kind of satisfying life. His most common device was that of the effects of the characters' past causes becoming manifest in one day. Few of his plays cover action lasting more than a day or two, creating a 'pressure-cooker' effect which is very compelling. His subject matter is profoundly serious – disease, despair, spiritual death, betrayal and hypocrisy among his themes – and many of his characters suffer for their fathers' sins. The great plays are essential reading – *A Doll's House, Hedda Gabler, The Master Builder, Ghosts, Rosmersholm* and *The Wild Duck*. The symbolism of his later *Little Eyolf* and *When We Dead Awaken* can be a little hard to take but it is worth reading *The Lady From The Sea, An Enemy Of The People* and *John Gabriel Borkman* if time permits.

AUGUST STRINDBERG, the other great Scandinavian writer, enjoyed a frenzied career, at first admiring and imitating Ibsen but later developing his own extraordinary style. While the subconscious feeds Ibsen's work, Strindberg was the first major writer actually to put the subconscious on stage. The Swedish dramatist was a mass of insecurities, hating women passionately, and often close to complete mental and physical collapse. He saw men and women in perpetual sexual conflict, with the woman as predator, a theme explored in *Miss Julie, Dance of Death,* and *The Father*. His influence on theatrical form was enormous, ignoring the conventional act and scene structure to 'imitate the inconsequential yet transparently logical shape of a dream. Everything can happen, everything is possible and probable. Time and place do not exist; on an insignificant basis of reality the imagination spins, weaving new patterns... The characters split, double, multiply, evaporate, condense, disperse, assemble. But one consciousness rules over them all, that of the dreamer.' The plays that most clearly show this revolutionary approach are **Dream Play, The Ghost Sonata** and the three parts of *To Damascus.*

ANTON CHEKHOV is the great Russian naturalist writer. In his plays, the words and actions of the characters are only the tip of the iceberg of a complex series of thoughts, feelings, relationships and desires. His characters are often self-deluding, always fully three dimensional. While the events in his plays may seem inconsequential, they reveal layer after layer of the character's soul. Chekhov is a passionate, funny, serious and ironic writer. He was a doctor by profession and a playwright by vocation. He brings an unjaundiced, unprejudiced eye to the actions and motivations of his characters with the precision of a great surgeon conducting an operation. The plays are brimful of real life and, whilst often moving, seldom fully tragic. He worked extensively with the revolutionary stage director, Konstantin Stanislavsky, whose training and directing methods have become part of the language of modern theatre. All Chekhov's full-length plays must be read – **The Seagull, Three Sisters, Uncle Vanya** and **The Cherry Orchard**. He died at the early age of 44, at his dacha in Yalta, the victim of tuberculosis.

The work of these playwrights, and their influence, took a while to reach the British public, who were outraged and disgusted when they were first exposed to such 'decadent filth.' In the meantime, Britain had produced one great writer of high comedy, **OSCAR WILDE** (1854-1900).

Wilde wrote brilliant Comedies of Manners, comparable with those of the Restoration period. Wilde, as famous for his life as his work, was only too aware of his talent. But he also said, in a reflective moment, "I have put my genius into my life, and only my talent into my writings." Wilde produced one flawless work – **The Importance Of Being Earnest**, an extraordinary comedy in which convention is stood on its head, the most absurd flights of fancy and twists of plot are treated with utter seriousness, and which has given the world Lady Bracknell's famous expostulation of outrage, 'A handbag?' His other plays are less perfect, using the melodramatic situations and dialogue common to the age, but are always leavened by Wilde's exquisite wit and epigrams. He is much taken with the notion of the 'woman with a past' and his characterisations of Mrs Cheveley in *An Ideal Husband*, Mrs Arbuthnot in *A Woman Of No Importance* and Mrs Erlynne in **Lady Windermere's Fan** are not free from sentimentality. *Salome* was banned in London when about to be produced starring Sarah Bernhardt. Wilde had written *Salome* in French, and the English translation was undertaken by his lover, Lord Alfred Douglas. Wilde was furious at the standard of the translation, which he called 'schoolboy', but this is the version which has come down to us and which is now accepted.

The first great English playwright of the nineteenth century, strongly influenced by Ibsen, was **GEORGE BERNARD SHAW** (1856-1950). As he lived to the age of 94, and continued writing plays up to his death, it is sometimes difficult to know whether to describe Shaw as a nineteenth or twentieth century playwright. Whichever definition one chooses, Shaw changed the face of English playwriting.

After a false start as a novelist, the young Shaw became a drama and music critic writing *The Quintessence of Ibsenism* (1891) and *The Perfect Wagnerite* (1898); then he turned to playwriting. He wrote some forty-five plays, from *Widowers' Houses* in 1885 to *Buoyant Billions* in 1948. He was an outspoken, unorthodox reformer, a Fabian socialist with a barbed wit and penetrating humour. His early plays attacked Victorian attitudes; rich landlords exploiting slum dwellings in *Widower's Houses*, the causes of prostitution in **Mrs. Warren's Profession** (1894), the romanticising of military heroes in **Arms and the Man** (1894), in which he, incidentally, created one of the most romantic of heroes. He further attacked the Salvation Army in **Major Barbara** (1905) and the medical profession in *The Doctor's Dilemma* (1906). The outraged indignation, abuse and censorship which this engendered led to difficulty in getting his plays performed, until Harley Granville-Barker presented a series of them at the Court Theatre between 1904 and 1907. Shaw gradually became recognised and respected as an important dramatist, for he had the ability to put both sides of an argument clearly and fairly. His lucid English is always leavened by wit, and he established that the play form could discuss any subject at all. His published plays have long prefaces, often not very relevant to the play itself but always stimulating. Privately, Shaw was a shy man, gentle, afraid of intimacy but generous and faithful in the few personal relationships he allowed himself. *Man and Superman* (1917), 'a comedy and a philosophy,' *Heartbreak House* (1917), which he described as his *King Lear*, and *Back to Methusalah* (1921), a "metabiological pentateuch" (five plays to be seen on five successive evenings) all set out his philosophy. The latter explores his conception of Creative Evolution, a Life Force saturating man, striving to improve and better mankind.

Another favourite theme was the deliberate pursuit by the ostensibly passive but actually positive female, hunting for the unsuspecting husband to guide and rule. Shaw's most popular plays are *Candida* (1895) and *Pygmalion* (1912), often revived and full of good speeches. *Heartbreak House* and *St. Joan* (1924) are regarded as his masterpieces.

Shaw has been accused of not creating real characters. Although it is true that his people are mouthpieces for his views, his speeches are not interchangeable between characters. A more apt criticism is that whereas the final act of a play ought to lead to a satisfactory solution of its conflict, Shaw's final acts mostly do not. His plays do not end, they simply stop. He epitomised his work in his own words: "my business as a classic writer of comedies is to chasten morals with ridicule... And I never do it without giving you plenty of laughing gas." Eventually he became world famous and was awarded the Nobel Prize for Literature in 1925. In 1928 he wrote *The Intelligent Woman's Guide to Socialism and*

Capitalism – a "Woman's" guide because he thought that women are more practical and sensible than men.

Shaw was not alone in his new drama, though his serious contemporaries could not match him. HENRY ARTHUR JONES (1851-1929), a prolific writer of both comedies and dramas about social problems, was a forceful believer in the importance of playwriting as a means of influencing people. Few of his plays are remembered. *The Liars* (1896) is by far his best and *Mrs Dane's Defence* (1900) contains a powerful third act of mounting tension, very impressive on stage. Jones tended to be melodramatic and to overdo the emotional content. He seems unable to draw out the logical conclusions of the problems he presented. However, his choice of themes marks him as one of the pioneers of modern drama. He wrote *The Renascence of English Drama* (1895) and *The Theatre of Ideas* (1915). He occupies a similar position to Tom Robertson, for they were both important influences on plays and theatre but not writers of any outstanding plays themselves.

HARLEY GRANVILLE-BARKER (1877-1946) was an actor, Shakespearean scholar and highly original producer. A valued friend of Shaw, Gilbert Murray and William Archer (a strong supporter of Ibsen and the new drama), he may be said to have established Shaw as a playwright. His productions of Shakespeare's plays paid scrupulous attention to the texts and to the variety and pace in the speaking of them. He set new standards for acting and production throughout Europe. His *Prefaces to Shakespeare*, analysing some ten plays from the director's point of view, are required reading for any actor or producer. He was not a prolific writer of plays but his *The Voysey Inheritance*, *The Marrying of Ann Leete* and *The Madras House* are well worth reading and still occasionally revived. With William Archer, Granville-Barker published *A National Theatre: Scheme and Estimates* in 1907, and they both continued, with Shaw, to advocate the establishment of a National Theatre. It was not until 1960, when all three were dead, that it was realised.

J. M. BARRIE (1861-1937) is noted for his whimsical and sentimental plays *Quality Street, The Admirable Crichton, What Every Woman Knows* and, of course, *Peter Pan* (Barrie's own projected wish that he had never grown up). He wrote a series of coy stories about *Thrums* for a small group he belonged to known as 'The Kailyard School'. ('Kailyard', a cabbage patch, derived from *'There is a bonny briar bush in our kailyard,'* a poem by Ian Maclaren). S.R. CROCKETT was another writer of this group.

JOHN GALSWORTHY (1867-1933 – see page 76) turned to literature after meeting Joseph Conrad, who called him a humanitarian moralist. His plays bluntly attack perceived injustice in a crisp, vigorous style. He was particularly sharp against the prejudices of the upper middle classes. *The Silver Box* (1906), *Strife* (1909– about an industrial dispute) and *The Skin Game* are representative of his plays. He did not present the causes of the ills he saw, as Shaw did. The only solution he could find was a plea for kindness and mercy, so his plays sometimes lack dramatic effect.

SIR ARTHUR PINERO (1859-1934) believed in the "well-made play". *Dandy Dick* (1887) was a well stage-managed farce on Victorian conventions, *The Second Mrs Tanqueray* (1893) a daring play for its time which today seems more melodrama than social criticism. Probably his finest play was *Trelawney of the Wells*, about the devotion of Rose Trelawney to the older, dying theatre.

Of some importance during the pre- and immediate post-World War period for both English and Irish literature was the outburst of creative activity in the Irish theatre. The Irish National Theatre Society was born in 1901 and, in turn, established the Abbey Theatre Company largely through W. B. Yeats, Lady Gregory and J. M. Synge. It was continued by Sean O'Casey. They took the everyday speech of Irish peasants and showed how it could be rhythmically, poetically and realistically used.

YEATS (see page 87-88) proved as influential a playwright as he was a poet, with verse plays based on Irish mythology.

The *Cuchulain Cycle* and *Cathleen ni Houlihan* will give a flavour of his style.

J. M. SYNGE (1871-1909) wrote powerfully of Irish peasant life in *Riders to the Sea, Playboy of the Western World* and *Deirdre of the Sorrows. Playboy* is the story of Christy Mahon, a weak and worthless man who becomes a hero because his boast that he has killed his father is believed. The language is tough and realistic, and the play told its audience things about the Irish psyche which they did not want to hear. There were riots in the theatre, but it is a beautifully constructed and still powerful play.

THE TWENTIETH CENTURY NOVEL

In this century, humanity's scientific powers over Nature, Space and the human body have advanced at a great pace, taking human history in hitherto unknown directions. Mankind, though, still finds it difficult to organise itself within a corporate state; to conduct relations with other states seems virtually unmanageable. There is a sense of fragmentation that dates back to the horrors of the First World War, after which the rapid rise and fall of movements, the ever-more frequent changes of fashion and the influence of new media such as film, television and good sound reproduction have all led to a rich but unclassifiable literature.

RUDYARD KIPLING (1865-1936) spans the years from the nineteenth to the twentieth century. Although he has fallen out of critical favour in recent years for his jingoism, his best poetry and prose deserves to be seriously considered. His poem *If* is deservedly a classic and many of his very rhythmic ditties are marvellously speakable. As a novelist he will live for his childrens' classics, *The Jungle Book, Kim* and *Just So Stories,* but to get the flavour of his adventure stories for adults, try *The Man Who Would Be King.* This is very representative of a genre which includes writers like H. RIDER HAGGARD (*King Solomon's Mines, She*) and SIR ARTHUR CONAN DOYLE (*The Lost World* and the *Sherlock Holmes* stories).

E. M. FORSTER (1879-1971) is a novelist of rare delicacy, writing with humour, passion and a potent eye for character and landscape. Many of his books (and particularly his short stories, many unpublished until after his death because of their explicit homosexuality) have a strong autobiographical content. This is probably less true of his twin masterpieces, **A Passage To India** and **Howard's End** with its plea that in relationships people should "only connect." His other work is always lively and interesting, often lighter than these two great works, and includes *A Room With A View, Where Angels Fear To Tread* and, published posthumously, *Maurice.*

JOHN GALSWORTHY (1867-1933) is famous for *The Forsyte Saga*, a magnificent but sprawling family saga that spans nine books and deals with the possessive instinct in man. The best three of these books are *The Man Of Property, In Chancery* and *To Let.* He was also a playwright of some note.

ARNOLD BENNETT (1867-1931) has fallen out of fashion in recent years, but he is a master of both construction and character, at least in his best novels. He is a storyteller par excellence and, though his style is sometimes turgid, the novels seldom fail to grip. The *Clayhanger* trilogy (***Clayhanger**, Hilda Lessways* and *These Twain*) epitomise his more serious style, set in the Potteries and concerning unspoken passions and misunderstandings. *Anna Of The Five Towns* is highly regarded, though the conclusion is unsatisfactory, while **The Old Wives' Tale** is a sympathetic and dramatic account of two sisters, spanning many years. His most approachable novel is the satirical **The Card**, which tells the comic tale of Denry Machin and his attempts at social climbing.

SOMERSET MAUGHAM (1874-1963) must be included because he is still widely read and enjoyed. He uses a small vocabulary and his sardonic style of writing is amusing and effective, confirming the fact that a good story is the best of all forms of literature. Profoundly cynical in his early books, he later developed a more kindly attitude to his fellow man. This development can be clearly seen by reading the short stories *Rain* and *Vessel of Wrath* and the novel *The Razor's Edge.* His best books were *Of Human Bondage, Cakes and Ale, The Moon and Sixpence,* and *The Summing Up.* The *Ashenden* stories are full of dramatic and human incident. He is probably the finest short story writer the twentieth century has produced.

H.G.WELLS (1886-1946) is now best known for his novels dealing with social problems, such as the popular *Kipps, Mr. Polly* and the lesser known *Love and Mr. Lewisham.*

He attacks the social problems of his time with sarcasm and he has a strong, idealistic view of what life could be like. Many of his books are concerned with imaginative developments in science and the future, such as *The First Men On The Moon* and *The Shape of Things To Come*, less exciting today as science has outstripped his forecast.

JAMES JOYCE (1882-1941), an Irish writer and major innovative force in modern literature, was a rebel against tradition and his own enviroment. He was a highly introverted man and took the novel along hitherto impossible channels, eventually having to invent his own language. The 'stream of consciousness' writing, ignoring conventional rules of grammar and syntax, has turned away many readers, although *The Dubliners* and **Portrait of the Artist as a Young Man** are very readable and essential for anyone who would seek to understand twentieth century writing. Some of the descriptive passage are magnificient. Read the 'Sermon on Hell' in *Portrait*, calculated to terrify all but the most sophisticated of readers, and compare it with Milton's Hell in *Samson Agonistes* and *Paradise Lost*, and read Stephen Daedalus' experience at the Retreat in Chapter Three. The style is intriguing, beginning with the baby language for Stephen's childhood (called mimetism – to mimic a child's mental reactions) and gradually developing language as he grows up. *Ulysses* is often regarded as the pivotal modern novel, a massive and detailed work following Stephen Daedalus around Dublin, parallelling the *Odyssey* of Homer. In this, and in his virtually incomprehensible last novel *Finnegan's Wake*, Joyce attempted to convey in writing the unconscious processes of the human mind.

VIRGINIA WOOLF (1883-1941) also developed a unique style and sense of language, describing events and characters in such minute detail that any sense of real time completely vanishes. She is much easier to read than Joyce but some readers find her mannered style irritating. Brave attempts are made to convey the stream of thoughts, sensations and attitudes that naturally occur to her individual characters. *Mrs. Dalloway* and **To the Lighthouse** should be read. Other novels that might be attempted include *Jacob's Room, Orlando* and *Between the Acts*. Woolf was married to Leonard Woolf, the founder of the Hogarth Press, and was a central figure of the so-called Bloomsbury Group, which included other writers (including Lytton Strachey), painters and assorted bohemians. Woolf's letters and diaries are of particular interest.

The celebrated **D.H.LAWRENCE** (1885-1930), often abused and always controversial, is a central and influential figure in modern literature. He was much influenced by Freud's writings on psychoanalysis, and felt that the puritanical culture of England was the basic cause of humanity's unhappiness. Like Freud, Lawrence sees sexual passion as being the core of all human activities. Like Joyce, Lawrence's work suffers from the reputation achieved for obscenity in a comparatively minor work, *Lady Chatterley's Lover*. The often autobiographical **Sons and Lovers** is a fine piece of writing, with its background of the Nottinghamshire coalfields, and paints a very moving picture of family relationships. His two most celebrated works, **The Rainbow** and **Women In Love** deal with two sisters, Ursula and Gudrun Brangwen, and their discovery of different facets of the world around them. Lawrence is often a little humourless, with no sense of absurdity but he has an astute command of English, clear and exact for his purposes. He could create atmosphere and convey an understanding of the inner self with startling clarity. He said that there is a struggle in everyone for a verbal consciousness of the inner life: 'every speck of protoplasm, every living cell is conscious, and all the time they give off a stream of consciousness which flows among the nerves and keeps us spontaneously alive.' He believed that parents' striving for communion through their children causes imbalance within the child and is responsible for difficulties in adolescence. Look at the two apparently trivial incidents in Chapter Nine of *Sons and Lovers*, the potato planting scene and the dive from the canal bridge; and the beautiful cathedral scene in Chapter Seven. Every incident in a Lawrence novel is directly related to the theme, which is what makes his work so artistically successful. His short stories are unusual and pleasurable, and his poetry will be discussed in the next chapter.

ALDOUS HUXLEY (1894-1963), a friend of Lawrence, was completely different in approach. His attack on society was ironic, as in the amusing satire *Antic Hay* and the rather more serious *Point Counter Point*, showing the growing disillusionment which followed the First World War. Later he became attracted to mysticism in *Eyeless in Gaza*. In his later books he introduced a new technique in the handling of time. His *Ape and Essence* is presented as a film scenario, another satire on the world after an atomic war. Towards the end of the 1930s and in the 40s and 50s Huxley became a didactic writer and, although eschewing the novel form, his books at this time remain important although sometimes difficult. *Themes and Variations*, although not a novel, is straightforward and a good book with which to begin reading Huxley. But also try *Grey Eminence*, a fascinating biography of one Father Joseph, mystic of the Roman church and, at the same time, a politician responsible for greatly prolonging the Hundred Years War. His descriptive passages are superbly written. His well-known satirical novel of the future, *Brave New World*, is worth comparing with Orwell's *1984*.

J.B.PRIESTLEY (1894-1979) is best known as a playwright (see page 97), but his novels of contemporary life, *The Good Companions* and *Angel Pavement* are highly regarded. Priestley is not as straightforward and simple as he is often assumed to be. There is a strain of mysticism running through his work, a subconscious seeking for perfection, what is now often referred to as transcendentalism.

One cannot ignore **GEORGE ORWELL** (1903-50), born Eric Blair. His essays and autobiographical writings are as important as his famous novels *1984* and *Animal Farm*, both of them satires on Stalinism and superbly constructed. Orwell was an acute observer of mankind, with many strongly held beliefs, and his style was spare, stylish and ironic. *Down And Out In Paris and London* and *The Road To Wigan Pier* are important historical documents in their own right, as well as entertaining reading. Try to find his essay *The Decline of the English Murder* which is worth comparing with Swift's *A Modest Proposal* and De Quincey's *On Murder As One Of The Fine Arts*.

EVELYN WAUGH (1903-66) was, by all accounts, an unpleasantly bombastic and arrogant man, and his snobbery and lack of understanding of women sometimes filters into his serious novels, making even the best of them flawed. ***Brideshead Revisited*** remains enormously popular, and certainly the first half of it is beautifully done, faltering only when it starts to deal seriously with Charles' relationship with Julia Flyte, who is thinly characterised. Waugh's satirical books are, however, in a class of their own, blackly comic, with outrageous but always human characters. ***Decline and Fall***, *Scoop, Vile Bodies, A Handful of Dust* and *The Ordeal of Gilbert Pinfold* are all worth reading.

MERVYN PEAKE (1911-1968) was a writer of Gothic imagination, capable of tremendous comedy and creating bizarre and disturbing characters, especially in the celebrated *Gormenghast* trilogy (*Titus Groan, Gormenghast* and the less satisfactory *Titus Alone*). *Gormenghast* is a fully realised fantasy about an almost recognisable other world. *Mr Pye* is lighter and charming, dealing with a good man's struggle against saintliness and ending with his transformation into an angel, wings and all, flying above the Channel Islands.

Other interesting writers of the first half of the century include ELIZABETH BOWEN, IVY COMPTON BURNETT and ELIZABETH GOUDGE (*A City of Bells* and *Green Dolphin Country*).

GRAHAM GREENE (1904-91) was a master of both form and style. He is a deceptively quiet writer of tremendous cumulative power and his best work is leavened with a tolerant irony that is very appealing. ***Brighton Rock***, his famous novel about the Brighton underworld, is as powerful today as on its first appearance in the 1940s. Greene's understanding of the human condition can be found in such diverse books as ***The Heart Of The Matter***, *The Quiet American,* ***The End of The Affair*** and the delightful ***Monsignor Quixote***, in which the action parallels Cervantes' classic, though with a Catholic priest and a Communist leader in the roles of Quixote and Sancho Panza.

KINGSLEY AMIS writes sour black comedies, and though his style is entertaining and witty, his characters are often deeply unpleasant. His more recent works, such as *The Old Devils* and *The Green Man* are as highly regarded as his earlier successes *Lucky Jim, Jake's Thing* and *The Riverside Villas Mystery.*

LAWRENCE DURRELL's famous *Alexandria Quartet* is a fascinating story, spread across four books – *Justine, Clea, Balthasar* and *The Mount of Olives.* As one reads on, one realises that the same story is being told from different points of view and the 'reality' of any given situation is profoundly coloured by the perceptions of whichever of the characters is observing it.

WILLIAM GOLDING is a master of language, most famous for his allegorical adventure story, *Lord Of The Flies* about a group of boys shipwrecked on an island. His other, less easily approachable work, includes *The Spire, Rites of Passage* and *Pincher Martin,* a fascinating tale about death and survival with some extraordinary imagery.

ANTHONY BURGESS cannot be ignored, for all his tendency to show his erudition and use a long word where a short one would do. He grew, apparently, sick and tired of the controversy created by a relatively minor work, *A Clockwork Orange* and his true quality can be found more in works like his massive *Earthly Powers, Any Old Iron* or the *Enderby* novels. He is greatly influenced by Joyce and his feel for the nuances of language is second to none.

PAUL SCOTT's ***The Raj Quartet*** is a fascinating portrait of post-war and newly independent India, in construction reminiscent of *The Alexandria Quartet.* It looks at every level of Anglo-Indian society in its telling of the rape of Daphne Manners and the unjust accusation of her lover, Hari Kumar. Memorable characters stalk its pages, most notably Merrick, a vicious but plausible policeman. Scott's other important work includes *Staying On*, a sort of postcript to *The Raj Quartet*, and *The Mark Of the Warrior*.

It is more difficult to write effectively of living novelists, though some have already achieved classic status and some have, even in the past twenty years, been through so many re-evaluations of their reputations that it is impossible to say whether their work will live on. The following comments, therefore, must be regarded with caution, though reading a selection would give one a good idea of the best in recent and contemporary writing.

ANTHONY POWELL's twelve-novel sequence, *A Dance To The Music Of Time*, is sometimes reminiscent of Proust, and is always elegant and entertaining.

IRIS MURDOCH is worth exploring. She writes with a strong narrative drive, a delicate sense of language and imagery and there are many layers to her work. Try *A Severed Head* or *The Sea, The Sea*.

MURIEL SPARK is a major writer of short, dense, elegantly written and superbly constructed, allusive prose. She is probably best known for **The Prime of Miss Jean Brodie** and *The Girls of Slender Means*, but is worth further exploration. Try *The Driver's Seat*, a short, ultimately bleak, but fascinating account of a woman's preparations for her own death, **The Takeover** with its references to the sympathetic magic of Frazer's *Golden Bough*, *Territorial Rights* and **Memento Mori**, a high comedy about a group of elderly friends reminded by telephone of their own mortality. Delicate, funny and delicious writing.

Of the 60s 'kitchen sink' writers, **DAVID STOREY**'s *Savile, Radcliffe, Pasmore* and *This Sporting Life*, ALAN SILLITOE's *Saturday Night and Sunday Morning* and *The Loneliness Of The Long Distance Runner*, STAN BARSTOW's *A Kind Of Loving*, and BARRY HINES' *Kes* (*A Kestrel For A Knave*) are all worth attention.

Some of the most interesting contemporary work is in the field of genre writing. The much despised crime novel has traditionally been excelled at by women writers. The two mistresses of the genre are P. D. JAMES (*Shroud For A Nightingale, Death Of An Expert Witness* and *An Unsuitable Job For A Woman*) and RUTH RENDELL, whose most brilliant writing occurs not in her popular Inspector Wexford novels, but in her psychological thrillers, such as *Live Flesh, The Tree Of Hands* and *Going Wrong*. Rendell also writes as **BARBARA VINE** and reveals herself as one of our finest, most thoughtful novelists in books like ***A Dark-Adapted Eye, Gallowglass*** and *A Fatal Inversion*.

MARTIN AMIS, son of Kingsley, is a major writer who deals with unpleasant subject matter and despicable characters in ironic, often scatological detail. His books are blackly funny, often offensive, always compelling and technically superb. *The Information*, ***Time's Arrow, London Fields, Money, Dead Babies*** and *Success* confirmed the precocious promise of *The Rachel Papers*.

PETER ACKROYD is another master of language and also explores the darker side of the human psyche, though in a kinder, more approachable way than Amis. ***Chatterton*** and ***Dan Leno and The Limehouse Golem*** are probably his best books to date. The latter is a multi-layered exploration not only of the young poet but of a contemporary loser trying to investigate his life. *Hawksmoor* is similarly complex, with a contemporary and seventeenth century story merging in the final pages.

SALMAN RUSHDIE cannot be ignored, though the fatwah placed upon him by Ayatollah Khomeini of Iraq, claiming that *The Satanic Verses* was blasphemous, has rather inflated his importance as a contemporary novelist. *Midnight's Children* is a more satisfying work.

KAZUO ISHIGURO, a Japanese novelist writing in English, has produced three novels of extraordinary beauty, compassion and constant surprises. The books are quiet and yet compelling. The true motives and past deeds of the central characters, however terrible or misguided, are leavened by an understanding of their motives. ***The Remains Of The Day*** is, arguably, the finest novel of the 1980s, but *An Artist Of the Floating World*, set in post-war Japan, is an almost equal achievement.

There are dozens of other recent and contemporary writers worth exploring. The list could be endless, but the following are worth exploring, including some major overseas twentieth century writers:

British and Canadian writers:

MARGARET ATWOOD – *The Handmaid's Tale*

WILLIAM BOYD – *The New Confessions, A Good Man In Africa, The Blue Afternoon*

ANITA BROOKNER – *Hotel Du Lac*

A.S. BYATT – *Possession, The Virgin In The Garden*

MARGARET DRABBLE – *The Waterfall*

DAPHNE DU MAURIER – *Rebecca, The House On the Strand, Jamaica Inn*

JOHN FOWLES – *The French Lieutenant's Woman, The Magus*

ALAN GARNER – *Red Shift*

WILLIAM HORWOOD – *Skallagrigg*

SUSAN HILL – *Strange Meeting, The Bird Of Night*

CHRISTOPHER ISHERWOOD – *Mr Norris Changes Trains, Goodbye To Berlin*

EDNA O'BRIEN – *The Country Girls, The Girl With Green Eyes*

BEN OKRI – *The Famished Road*

BARBARA PYM – *No Fond Return Of Love, Excellent Women*

MARY RENAULT – *The Persian Boy, The Charioteer, The Mask of Apollo*

LISA ST AUBAN DE TERAIN – *The Tiger*

PAUL THEROUX – *The Mosquito Coast, The Family Arsenal*

ROSE TREMAIN – *The Swimming Pool Season, Restoration*

MARY WESLEY – *The Camomile Lawn, Harnessing Peacocks*

ANTONIA WHITE – *Frost In May*

Australian and New Zealand writers:

KERI HULME – *The Bone People*

THOMAS KENEALLY – *Schindler's Ark, The Chant of Jimmie Blacksmith*

European writers:

ALBERT CAMUS – *The Stranger, The Plague*

COLETTE – *Cheri, Gigi,* the *Claudine* novels

UMBERTO ECO – *The Name Of The Rose, Foucault's Pendulum*

ALBERTO MORAVIA – *Two Women, The Woman Of Rome*

VLADIMIR NABOKOV – *Lolita, Laughter In The Dark*

JEAN PAUL SARTRE – *Roads To Freedom*

American writers:

WILLIAM FAULKNER – *As I Lay Dying, Absolom,Absolom, Requiem For A Nun*

F. SCOTT FITZGERALD – *The Great Gatsby, Tender Is The Night*

ERNEST HEMINGWAY – *A Farewell To Arms, The Sun Also Rises*

NORMAN MAILER – *The American Dream, Ancient Voices*

TONI MORRISON – *Beloved*

PHILIP ROTH – *Portnoy's Complaint*

J.D. SALINGER – *Catcher In The Rye*

GORE VIDAL – *1876, Myra Breckinridge, Hollywood*

ALICE WALKER – *The Color Purple, The Third Life of Grange Copeland*

TWENTIETH CENTURY POETRY

New forms in composition, presentation and syntax are common to the twentieth century, and the fragmentation of the modern psyche is reflected in the exploration of free verse forms. There was much new and exciting work in the first half of the century but it took the popular poets of the 1960s to bring poetry back into general circulation. Most of the anthologies of Twentieth Century Verse, by reason of their publication date, favour the poets of the first half of the century but these alone bear witness to the number of poets worth reading. *The Faber Book of Modern Verse* gives no fewer than sixty-six poets; Cox and Dyson in *Poems of this Century* (Edward Arnold) give forty (not all of them duplicating Faber) and even George MacBeth, very selective in his *Poetry 1900-1965* (Longman and Faber) still considers twenty-two important. A varied selection should be read, and the undoubted major poets listed below in **bold** type must not be ignored.

W.B. YEATS (1865-1939), like Hardy, straddles the late Victorian age and the early twentieth century, yet he is the more 'modern' of the two. Yeats has been called England's greatest poet since Wordsworth (continuing the tradition of great Irish writers being 'stolen' and incorporated into the English canon). He is a lyricist, emotional and even mystical, and he developed a dignified grandeur. He achieved a reputation as director of the Abbey Theatre in Dublin, Ireland's National Theatre. Yeats is more positive than Hardy, seeking a religion for all mankind. In *Anima Mundi* he says that 'thoughts and emotions are often but spray flung up from the hidden guide that follows a mood that no eye can see.' Much of his writing comes from the intuitive part of the mind, anticipating psycho-analysis and psychology. Yeats constantly refers to the 'unknown instructor' intervening in our lives, although he gives no indication of who or what that instructor is. *The Second Coming* illustrates this. Try, too, *The Long-Legged Fly* with its yearning for the silence of creativity,

Mad as the Mist and Snow, *Beautiful and Lofty Things* (with tongue in cheek), *The Lake Isle of Innisfree*, the complex sonnet *Leda and the Swan* and the longer *Dialogue of Self and Soul*. As Yeats grew older, he sometimes seems to reject any notion of man and woman other than as simple, desiring animals, and the responsibilities of politics – particularly Anglo-Irish politics, exercised him throughout his career.

Yeats stood alone, but the first great flowering of inescapably twentieth century poetry came about as a result of the First World War. Of these, the greatest poet is probably **WILFRED OWEN** (1893-1918), tragically killed in action in the last week of the war, before he could complete his book of poems. They were published posthumously in 1920 and immediately caught the public's attention, particularly two – *Anthem For Doomed Youth* and *Strange Meeting*. The latter, with its famous conclusion,

> I am the enemy you killed, my friend
> I knew you in this dark; for so you frowned
> Yesterday through me as you stabbed and killed.
> I parried; but my hands were loath and cold.
> Let us sleep now...

is both moving and the epitome of war poetry. In the preface to the book he never saw, he wrote, 'My subject is war, and the pity of war. The poetry is in the pity.' This is as accurate a definition of his work as that of any scholar.

RUPERT BROOKE (1887-1915) was one of the first casualties of the war and retains a strong sense of Edwardian England and patriotism. His romanticism reflects the mood of young men in the early part of the war, before disillusion and horror crept in. Try *The Soldier* and *The Old Vicarage, Grantchester*.

ISAAC ROSENBERG (1890-1918), another war casualty, was experimental in his poetry, and he used his Jewish background to powerful effect. Try *August 1914* or *Louse Hunt*. **SIEGFRIED SASSOON** (1886-1967) lived on long after the conflict but he is best remembered for the work of those years, such as the powerful sonnet *Attack*, the moving *Everyone Sang* and *The General.* Of his later work, try *Sporting Acquaintances, Two Old Ladies* and *When I'm Alone.* Michael Meyer, the distinguished translator of Ibsen and Strindberg, tells of a youthful visit to Sassoon, who was more concerned with cricket than comfort. After a poor lunch, Sassoon took the young Meyer to his study and spoke of Wilfred Owen. "I've some letters here," he said and passed him Owen's last letter from the Front. In it, Owen said he had just written a poem and would like Sassoon's opinion. Meyer turned the page and there, in Owen's faded handwriting, were the words, *'It seemed that out of battle I escaped...'* – the opening of *Strange Meeting.*

ROBERT GRAVES (1895-1990) is not only a lyric poet of great sensitivity and passion, but his prose writings embraced the novel, autobiography and philosophy. Of his poems try *A Welsh Incident, The Cool Web, Nature's Lineaments* and *It Was All Very Tidy.* His autobiography, *Goodbye To All That* vividly covers his experiences in the trenches in the First World War, and his famous historical novels, *I, Claudius* and *Claudius The God* are among the best of the genre.

ROBERT BRIDGES (1844-1930) was Poet Laureate at the time of the outbreak of the war. Although his output includes some war poetry, he is best remembered for his lyrical poems and his interest, foreshadowing Eliot, in the spiritual needs of the age. *A Passer-By* and *London Snow* are representative.

Another poet killed during that First War was **EDWARD THOMAS** (1878-1917), already 36 when the conflict began. His work shows a loving and accurate observation of the English pastoral scene and few of his poems are directly about war. He searches out feelings in a hesitant yet precise way, and there is a mysticism underlying the apparent plainness of his style. *Old Man, Cock-Crow, Out In The Dark* and *The Mill-Pond* all repay study.

After the war romantic idealism was dead, smothered by the senseless slaughter and the vileness of the trenches. The prevailing mood was confused, angry, bitter and despairing.

T. S. ELIOT (1888-1964) was one of the most educated of poets, studying in America, France and England. He thought highly of Dryden, whom he said first established 'a normal English speech valid for both verse and prose' and he was much influenced by the metaphysical John Donne. His work really divides into three periods. The first was one of disillusion, even disgust, with the unlovely world following the First World War. His mood became rather more optimistic after his conversion to High Church Christianity, which resulted in a belief in man living concurrently 'in time' and 'in eternity.' In this period he advocated that the disillusions of this world are less important when viewed against the great sweep of time. The third period saw him as a dramatist (see page 99), seeking, somewhat intellectually, 'to justify the ways of God to man', and therefore reminiscent of Milton.

His early despair is clearly seen in *The Love Song of J. Alfred Prufrock* (1917), in which he uses flat, undistinguished, everyday speech to show his hopeless acceptance of the triviality of everday life, a theme taken up in *The Hollow Men* (1925). His most important work, possibly the seminal poem of the century, is *The Waste Land* (1922), a series of visions covering centuries of chaos in the world of time and space. In it, Eliot translated ancient myths into the contemporary world and expressed man's need for, and yet fear of, salvation. It is a difficult, cryptic poem, easy enough to read but with allusions and half-quotations that are often baffling to the ordinary reader. Indeed, Eliot had to write his own commentary on it. *Journey of the Magi* and *A Song of Simeon* belong to the second period, as do the more positive *Ash-Wednesday* and *Four Quartets*. The latter is the masterpeice of the second period, which saw the development of a taut, lyrical style. The *Quartets* are meditations on eternity, and are deeply influenced by Eliot's Christianity, a faith he embraced with all the passionate fervour of a convert. There are eminently speakable pieces, too, in *Poems Written in Early Youth* and *Old Possum's Book of Practical Cats*. Eliot would have been amused by the musical show *Cats* made from some of his pieces. He was a brilliant essayist and critic in *Poetry and Poets* (1957), a very influential work affecting many who followed him.

The next group of poets, (Auden, Day-Lewis, MacNeice and Spender) wrote first of the economic depression and spiritual crisis of the 1930s, the sickness of society expressed by Eliot, but they offered a different solution. They are often referred to as 'the neo-metaphysicals', harking back to Donne. They substituted for the earlier metaphysicals' salvation through Christ an acceptance of the Marxist analysis of society and 'salvation through socialism.' They expressed it with vitality and enthusiasm, experimenting with metrical forms, rhythms and a 'nature' seen as the squalid, dirty and impersonal factories of the Midlands. They had difficulty, however, in putting their despair and their idealism into such persuasive verse as Eliot and Hopkins. They could not bridge the ever-existent breach between the poet and his reader, what D. M. David called 'the disjunction between himself and his audience.' Later they became more individual and personal, thus more effective.

W. H. AUDEN (1907-1973) is the most important of the four, and, together with Eliot, the outstanding figure of his time. Satirising capitalist society, Auden drew attention to the man dominated by machines, expressing the squalor and misery of the mass unemployment of the 1930s. He argued with lucidity the spiritual bankruptcy of the decade. His *Age of Anxiety* (1948) gave a popular title to the attitudes of the time. Auden is an intellectual poet, his intellect sometimes getting in the way of felt and experienced emotion. His real interest was in the nature of man himself; he was concerned with social and political affairs in so far as they reflected man's own nature; he was aware of man's solitariness in the universe – to be born, to live and die alone. He often called his poems 'squares and oblongs' to reflect the harshness, sharpness and inconsequentiality of the modern world as he saw it – without feeling for people, only for material objects.

His fundamental theme, in his maturity, was 'we must love one another or die', spiritually as well as physically. Original and interesting in the use of imagery, his intellectual approach nonetheless reveals areas of great sensitivity and passion. Read *Lullaby, Musée Des Beaux Arts, In Memory of W.B. Yeats, Look, Stranger, Consider this,* and *Lady Weeping at the Cross Roads.*

C.DAY-LEWIS (1904-1973) was the most lyrical, civilised and visionary of the four, as can be seen in *As One Wanders into all Workings, You that Love England,* and *The Conflict.* STEPHEN SPENDER (b1909) was more concerned with subjective lyrical meditation as in *Edge of Being,* a metaphysical poem on the nature of beauty. *In Railway Halls, The Pylons* and *The Landscape Near an Aerodrome* are representative of his work. LOUIS MACNEICE (1907-1963) was sensuous, bright and melancholy in turn, often using dancing rhythms. His work is highly coloured, but sometimes clumsily expressed. Try *Perseus, The Sunlight in the Garden, Prognosis* and *Prayer Before Birth.*

EDWIN MUIR (1887-1959) was both poet and scholar. His best work is quiet and intimate, with a thoughtful, almost melancholy air. Try *Suburban Dream, Horses, Love's Remorse* or *The Combat.*

D. H. LAWRENCE, as well as being an important novelist, is one of the twentieth century's major poets. He tended to write quite long poems, in a free verse form, and his use of language and assonance is remarkably effective. There is no sentimentality in Lawrence's poetry, as there sometimes is in his novels, and they are very effective when spoken aloud, because of this very directness. Read *Snake, Bavarian Gentians, The Best of School* and perhaps *Money Madness.*

Other modern novelists who have written effective poetry include MERVYN PEAKE (*I cannot give the reasons*), KINGSLEY AMIS (*A Dream of Fair Women, Something Nasty In The Bookshop*) and LAWRENCE DURRELL (*A Prospect of Children, This Unimportant Morning, A Portrait of Theodora*).

The celebrated Welsh roisterer **DYLAN THOMAS** (1914-53) is best known for his play for voices, ***Under Milk Wood***. He was a poet of resonance and richness, the romantic, angry music of the Welsh valleys translated into words on the page. His themes were intense; sex, birth, death and nostalgia for lost childhood. There is much vitality in Thomas, though his imagery is sometimes obscure. ***Do not go gently into that good night, The force that through the green fuse drives the flower***, *Fern Hill* and *It is the sinners' dust-tongued bell* will give you a flavour of both the man and his works.

In contemporary poetry, there is an increased use of syllabic metres with no fixed number of stresses to the line, the sense usually determining them. This began as far back as the 1930s but has gained great momentum since 1945. More free verse is written, depending for its rhythms on the grouping of phrases (often indicated by the punctuation) rather than on syllables and lines. Thought, mood, and atmosphere are much more compressed and the imagery more complex, requiring greater attention for understanding. The greatest change of all is the broadening of subject matter – politics, social habits, psychological problems and the use of everyday events in people's lives. Nor does the poet any longer stand outside his subjects looking on; instead he is now increasingly involved with his subjects and wants the reader to be so involved.

PHILIP LARKIN's (1922-) poetry is tinged both with melancholy and irony, a sometimes startling combination. He is very accessible, with a strong sense of narrative, and his broader themes are always grounded in paticularities. He appreciates the human hunger for ritual and form. Read ***Mr Bleaney, Church Going***, *The Explosion, Myxomatosis, MCMXIV, At Grass, Deceptions* and *Going.*

TED HUGHES (b1930) is a Yorkshireman and was married, at one point, to the major American poet, **SYLVIA PLATH** (1932-63). Hughes has great energy, forceful syntax and imagery, stressing Nature's vitality and endurance. His ***Horses***, a striking poem, might well be compared with Edwin Muir's *The Horses* and with Philip Larkin's *At Grass*. ***Hawk***

Roosting, Relic, An Otter, Snowdrop and the longer and frightening *The Brother's Dream* are representative of Hughes. Of his later work, the collections *Crow* and *Wodwo* contain some magnificent work. He becomes involved with his characters and there is nothing sentimental or lush in his writing. Plath was an insecure person, who committed suicide, and her poems have a dangerous, dark edge to them. The sense of paranoia is strong, expressed not only in her poems but in her fascinating novel, *The Bell-Jar.* The bleakness of her subject matter and tone is off-set by a marvellous sense of form and language, expressed in such poems as *Childless Woman, Crossing The Water, Mushrooms* and *The Arrival of the Bee Box.*

A major English poet, who also committed suicide, was **STEVIE SMITH** (1902-71). She lived a quiet, secluded life with her aunt in North London, and her writing reflects the despair and fantasies that lurk under the surface of the apparently ordinary. This is vividly illustrated in *Not Waving But Drowning* and *My Hat.* There is much humour and tolerance of human frailty in Smith's work, which often drives sudden, sharp splinters of pain into the reader's heart. Try also *Bog-Face* and *The Jungle Husband.*

THOM GUNN's precision, grace, elegance, energy and, sometimes, violence, are attractive. His syllabic writing compares favourably with Marianne Moor's. *Black Jackets, The Wound, On the Move, Considering the Snail* and *My Sad Captain* indicate his methods.

JOHN BETJEMAN (1906-84) is a poet of great charm and a surprising degree of substance. His subject matter is the small, the ordinary and eccentric and his verse forms are traditional and beautifully balanced. Above all, Betjeman is celebrated for his humour and his poems about childhood and innocence, not necessarily the same thing. His autobiographical poem *Summoned By Bells* should be read, along with *Diary Of A Church Mouse, NW5 & N6, Miss Joan Hunter Dunn, Death In Leamington* and perhaps *Meditation on the A30* and *Senex.*

There was a movement of popular poetry which, like so much else of popular culture, exploded from Liverpool during the 1960s. Of this great surge of work, the three writers who have remained major are **BRIAN PATTEN, ROGER MCGOUGH** and ADRIAN HENRI. Theirs is a laconic, ironic and wry humour, lying on the surface of great seriousness and, sometimes anger. McGough's *Every day* encapsulates the mood and tone:

> Every day
> I think about dying.
> About disease, starvation,
> violence, terrorism, war,
> the end of the world.
>
> It helps
> Keep my mind off things.

Of McGough, the most whimsical of the three, try also *The Lesson, Summer With Monika, Snipers, He Who Owns The Whistle* and *At Lunchtime, A Story of Love.* Brian Patten is the most serious of the three, representative works being *Meat, The Schoolboy, **Something That Was Not There Before**, Sleep Now* and *Ode On Celestial Music.* Of Henri try *The Triumph Of Death, Spring Song For Mary* and *Batpoem.*

ELIZABETH JENNINGS (b1926) is another poet who uses traditional metre and form in many of her poems. Her apparent simplicity and quietness should not blind one to the thoughtful depths she explores in such poems as *In The Night, For A Child Born Dead, Fountain* and *My Grandmother.*

Of other poets, THEODORE ROETHKE's *The Far Field, Cuttings*, and *I Knew a Woman*, R.S. THOMAS' *Here, On the Farm* and *Blackbird Singing* and JOHN WAIN's *This Above All is Precious and Remarkable* and *On the Death of a Murderer*, are examples of the modern poet's search for honesty, in a variety of forms. TONY HARRISON is a controversial poet and playwright, often angry and violent in tone, and such works as *V* repay study.

MEDGH McGLUCKIAN seems a most attractive poet, using odd metaphors. She is unafraid of obscurity, and her work calls for thought and effort in unravelling the layers of meaning. Her *The Flower Master* is an intriguing collection of pieces. MHAIRI O'NEILL is also work exploring, as is PHOEBE HESKETH.

ROY FULLER is a poet who wrote on sociological themes with the accuracy of description one would expect from a solicitor. His *Collected Poems* (1962) is considered to contain his best work. CHRISTOPHER MIDDLETON follows in the tradition set by Eliot, and PETER PORTER, a poet of the 60s, is witty in his condemnation of society. *Your Attention Please* is an example of his good work. W. S. MERWIN's two pieces in the *Faber Book of Modern Verse* are worth looking at and GEORGE MacBETH has written some arresting verse.

Other recent and contemporary writers you may find attractive, including some major American writers (strictly outside the scope of this guide and marked *) are:

GEORGE BARKER (*To My Mother, Sonnet of Fishes*)

ROY CAMPBELL (*Horses on the Camargue*)

* e e cummings (*anyone lived in a pretty how town, The Mouse, Two X*)

JOHN DRINKWATER (*Mad Tom Tatterman*)

WILLIAM EMPSON (*This Last Pain, Aubade*)

* ROBERT FROST (*After Apple-picking, Stopping By Woods On A Snowy Evening*)

* ROBERT LOWELL (*Alfred Corning Clark, Child's Song*)

JOHN MASEFIELD (*A Consecration, Cargoes*)

MARIANNE MOORE (*The Steeple-jack, Silence*)

* OGDEN NASH (*Song to be Sung by the Father of Infant Female Children*)

* EZRA POUND (*The River Merchant's Wife: A Letter, The Seafarer*)

CLIVE SANSOM (*The Witnesses, Sorcerer*)

EDITH SITWELL (*The King of China's Daughter*)

ALAN TATE (*Horatian Epode to the Duchess of Malfi, The Oath*)

TWENTIETH CENTURY DRAMA

The early twentieth century saw so many good playwrights, writing in a variety of styles, that is it difficult not to relate them back to the men who laid the groundwork – Ibsen, Shaw and Wilde.

In Ireland, **SEAN O'CASEY** (1884-1964) inherited the Abbey Theatre from Yeats and Synge and produced powerful plays, often with the political upheavals of Ireland as the backdrop. O'Casey's plays are compassionate and earthy, with fully alive characters. *Juno and the Paycock, The Plough and the Stars, The Shadow Of A Gunman* and *The Star Turns Red* are all essential reading.

In England, the well-made play continued to dominate the commercial theatre – which was its spiritual home until after the theatrical upheavals of the 1950s. SOMERSET MAUGHAM (1874-1965 – see page 76) was a skilful craftsman in stage technique, his plays remaining popular today. Witty, with his usual sardonic, cynical humour, he mistrusted contemporary virtues and delighted in contradicting them. Like Wilde, he wrote comedies of manners, though he lacked Wilde's lightness of touch. There was always a hint of cruelty in his writing. The plots are always interesting and come to satisfactory and appropriate endings, always within the conventions of the commercial theatre. *The Circle* and *The Constant Wife* are still amusing.

J. B. PRIESTLEY (see page 79), very much a man of letters and a public figure, tried to give new depths to drama, constantly experimenting with new devices. *Dangerous Corner* is an ingeniously constructed play with a powerful final scene which is almost a repetition of the opening. *When We Are Married*, a farce, *An Inspector Calls*, a modern morality play, and the idealistic *They Came to a City* all show his unusual approach to playwriting. He is famous for his experiments with time (derived from J. W. Dunne's *An Experiment with Time*) and the plays which exploit this include **Time and the Conways**, *I Have Been Here Before* and *Johnson Over Jordan*, the latter not very successful commercially but one of his best plays. Priestley believed in simple goodness and that, if properly treated, people will prefer to be good.

NOEL COWARD (1899-1973), actor, singer, composer, playwright, had an excellent stage sense, showing that the simplest scenes could be theatrically effective. He was popularly known as 'The Master' and in his best plays he showed himself the equal of Wilde at brittle, sophisticated comedies of manners about the leisured classes. He also wrote well on patriotic subjects, particularly during the 1939-45 war. He was by turns sentimental, frivolous, trivial, impudent, amoral and tended to characterize thinly, giving great scope for the actors to give star performances. Coward adopted a clipped, staccato speech and was careful never to offend. Read **Hay Fever**, **Blithe Spirit**, a perfect farce, and **Private Lives**, his most successful play. He began his meteoric career in 1924 with a serious play about a son's relationship with his mother, *The Vortex*. It was a huge *succes de scandale*, made Coward himself a star and, interestingly, his understudy was John Gielgud, later to be one of the great actors of the century. *Private Lives*, too, saw one of the early performances of Laurence Olivier in a supporting role. Coward fell out of fashion after the war, but his career as a cabaret artiste and film actor continued unabated.

There were a host of other playwrights in the commercial theatre, most of them forgotten already, but the First World War drama, *Journey's End* by R.C. SHERRIFF, and *On Approval*, a slight Wildean comedy by FREDERICK LONSDALE are still revived. The best craftsman of the well-made play, after Priestley, was undoubtedly **TERENCE RATTIGAN** (1911-1980). Beginning with inconsequential farces like *French Without Tears*, he soon showed a considerable ability in writing dialogue. He was honest in claiming only to write conventionally, but he did write occasionally on serious subjects in such plays as *Separate Tables, The Browning Version* and *The Deep Blue Sea*, in which he explored the middle-class soul with great compassion.

The poets, T.S. ELIOT and W.H. AUDEN, together with CHRISTOPHER ISHERWOOD and CHRISTOPHER FRY all sought to revive the verse play during the thirty years up to 1960. Eliot had some difficulty distinguishing between verse for speaking as verse and verse for speaking in a play. His best piece of dramatic writing was *Sweeney Agonistes*, of which only a fragment now remains. Eliot said that he wanted verse plays to conform as nearly as possible to the rhythms of ordinary speech, and in the essay *Poetry and Drama* discussed the difficulties of reviving poetic drama. In 1935, *Murder in the Cathedral* and in 1939 *The Family Reunion* were both successful, powerful and effective in production. *The Cocktail Party* and *The Elder Statesman* found Eliot in difficuties coalescing verse speaking with natural everyday conversation.

Auden and Isherwood also experimented with verse forms in *The Dog Beneath the Skin*, with music by Benjamin Britten, "a metaphysical satirical extravaganza on fairy-tale themes and current musical comedy, amusing but limited". *The Ascent of F6* is a powerful, symbolic play on social and psychological themes, haunting and compelling.

Christopher Fry wrote immediately after the second World War. He began with *A Phoenix Too Frequent* and *The Lady's Not For Burning* in 1949, both highly successful. He followed this with *Venus Observed* and a prose translation of Jean Anouilh's *L'Invitation au Chateau* which he called *Ring Round the Moon*. It is fashionable to dismiss Fry as merely a master of pretty verbiage but his plays are full of wit, poetic conceits, a strain of mysticism and beautifully controlled language. His *A Sleep of Prisoners* is a serious play, effective in the theatre but even more telling in a church where it can become moving and alarming. *Boy with a Cart* and *Curtmantle* are gentle and well-constructed.

THE 'KITCHEN SINK' REVOLUTION

1956 was the year of the Suez Crisis, Elvis Presley and *Look Back In Anger* by **JOHN OSBORNE,** the single most influential play of the century. First performed at the Royal Court, the home of the most innovative and challenging drama for the next twenty years, Osborne's play gave voice to the 'angry young man', dissatisfied with the dreary living conditions of Austerity Britain. For the first time, the young found themselves presented to themselves on stage. Working class and regional experience were to be the theme of most of the major drama for the next ten years. *Look Back In Anger* is not a great play, for Osborne's sense of dramatic structure is weak and he has a tendency to make the same point three or four times, but it marked the break with the drawing-room comedy and drama which had dominated the theatre up until that point. All his plays are structurally flawed, but he can write magnificent, passionate speeches. Try *Luther,* *The Entertainer, A Patriot For Me* and *Inadmissible Evidence.* These plays also brought to the fore a new breed of contemporary actor, again often from regional and working-class backgrounds, such as Albert Finney, Tom Courtenay, Peter O'Toole and Nicol Williamson.

The plays that followed Osborne's lead were of mixed quality, virile and restless, presenting a profusion of new theatrical experiences. The barriers were down, and there were enough exciting writers to ensure that they stayed down. The year before *Look Back In Anger* changed the face of British theatre, **SAMUEL BECKETT's** *Waiting for Godot* opened at the Arts Theatre, an intellectual, funny, uneventful play which explored the relationship of two tramps who were, literally, 'waiting for Godot' to arrive. He never does arrive, and the play brilliantly and poignantly explores a state of mind. Played on a bare stage, except for one solitary tree, it sees the two hopeless tramps struggle with words to find an identity. We do not know who Godot is. Beckett is careful to let us think what we will of him, real or imaginery, or perhaps he is just a name. The play has neither plot nor message. The characters have an affinity with Chekhov's helpless characters, yearning for what they cannot have. For the first time since Strindberg we are confronted with the idea that a play need not have plot, theme or meaning in the accepted sense of the word. It may be like a piece of music or an abstract painting, simply an experience. To explore Beckett further, look at *Endgame*, with its characters popping up out of dustbins, a comment upon human waste. ***Happy Days*** is about a woman gradually buried up to her neck, able to do nothing but talk to "break the silence". Beckett's plays call to mind the comment of JEAN PAUL SARTRE in *Existentialism and Humanism* that "The existentialist finds it extremely embarrassing that God does not exist, for there disappears with Him all possibility of finding values in an intelligible heaven". Other work includes *Krapp's Last Tape* and *Not I.*

Osborne and Beckett were the pioneers, Beckett remaining outside the mainstream of playwriting throughout his career. Of the writers who followed in such profusion, many have proved to be better craftsmen than Osborne, though some, like SHELAGH DELANEY (*A Taste of Honey*), ROBERT BOLT (*A Man For All Seasons*) and ANN JELLICOE (*The Knack*) proved to be one-play wonders. Delaney's play shows, in a realistic situation, the growth of a schoolgirl in uncongenial surroundings, a pointed attack on squalid social circumstances. It is a direct working class protest against the false conventions of the commercial theatre. Very closely observing life in a working class suburb of Manchester, its bitterness and disorder is counterpointed by an idyllic love affair.

Another writer of the period with working class themes is JOHN ARDEN (b1930) who also wrote a number of plays with his wife, MARGARETTA D'ARCY. Arden's *Live Like Pigs* is a rowdy, violent play setting vagrant squatters in conflict with "respectable" people. Arden is more greatly admired than both Osborne and Wesker for his prose, verse and experimentation with form. *Sergeant Musgrave's Dance* is his best play, a study in the meaning of violence and a dramatic parable on the degrading bestiality of war. He suggests that meeting force with force is self-defeating. *The Workhouse Donkey* is about local council corruption. A fair comment on Arden's plays is that they tend to lack tension and are driven along by political passion rather than stagecraft.

ARNOLD WESKER (b1932) is of working class origin and is a political activist. His trilogy, *Chicken Soup With Barley, Roots* and *I'm Talking About Jerusalem* shows him a better writer than Osborne, for the restlessness, frustration, disappointment and protest come through with more force. The plays trace a family from the East End of London searching for the ideal life over twenty years from 1936. They form a history of disillusionment, although individual characters are not without growth. *Chips With Everything* is a symbolic attack on the British class war and contains one remarkable mimed scene. Wesker's plays have natural settings and no special effects. All the interest is concentrated on the characters. There are well-made small scenes, very actable, and individual speeches are very speakable. Wesker's work showed an enormous potential which does not seem to have developed, and he has not written anything of any impact for some years.

PETER SHAFFER (b1926), however, has retained his grip on the popular imagination. *Five Finger Exercise*, two years after *Look Back in Anger*, is a family drama expressing the uncertainties and discontents of a new generation in conflict with the old. It deals with homosexuality sympathetically by contemporary standards, but looks weak and dated now. Shaffer's later work is much more interesting. The breadth of his choice of subject matter and style, together with the consistency of his writing, mark him as an important – and latterly very commercial – dramatist. He has an objectivity remarkably effective on stage. ***The Royal Hunt of the Sun*** is more of a pageant than a play, dealing with the sixteenth century Spanish expedition to Mexico to subdue and conquer the Incas of Peru. *Equus* is a combination of intellectual psychological argument (not altogether original or accurate) with stunning theatrical effects. The speeches Shaffer writes for Dysart, a psychiatrist dealing with the disturbed Alan Strang, mark Shaffer as a master dramatist. His next play, *Amadeus*, was weaker but commercially more successful, and his **Lettice and Lovage** is a superb high comedy.

HAROLD PINTER (b1930) is probably the key dramatist of his generation and one who continues to provoke controversy, though he has not written anything of note since 1980. He is famed for the sense of unease and danger he creates. His characters find themselves in situations which are dangerous and unfamiliar (though unspecified) and in which they seek to anchor themselves by language. Pinter is famed for his adroit use of pause and silence which, with the accompaniment of beautifully observed commonplace dialogue, can cause laughter or fear. He has an affinity with Beckett, the same keen ear for the quirks of the spoken word. Interestingly, his characters have moved up the social scale over the years, as Pinter himself has become richer and more successful. His early plays include **The Caretaker, The Lover, The Birthday Party** and **The Homecoming**, and of his later work, **Old Times** and **Betrayal** are very impressive.

DAVID STOREY (b1933) writes entertainingly and interestingly on family and moral problems in a naturalistic style. *In Celebration* (1969) is about three sons returning home for their parents' wedding anniversary and finding their new lives incompatible with their parents' expectations. *Home* (1970) finds two "friends" and two women telling each other stories, true or untrue, until one perceives that they are in some kind of a mental home, in which the audience are the other inmates! They realise that God is disappointed with His world and may well begin again elsewhere. There is much comedy found in this potentially depressing subject.

PETER NICHOLS (b1927) writes black comedy – very serious themes treated as comedy, because to treat them seriously would be too harrowing, epitomising the old adage that laughter is close to tears. *A Day in the Death of Joe Egg* (1967) is about how a young couple cope with a child suffering from cerebral palsy. *The National Health* (1969) takes place in a hospital and derives humour from illness, even death. In both plays euthanasia is much discussed. Subsequent plays by Nicholas have not been as successful, though critically acclaimed. *Passion Play* (1978) is about the bewilderment and suffering of marital infidelity, *Poppy* a musical play about the opium trade and *Born In The Gardens* a play about an impossible mother and family relationships, set in his native Bristol.

Of the Americans. one cannot ignore the massive achievements of **EUGENE O'NEILL** (1888-1953 – *Long Day's Journey Into Night, Desire Under The Elms, Mourning Becomes Electra*), **TENNESSEE WILLIAMS** (1914-1976 – *A Streetcar Named Desire, The Glass Menagerie, Cat On A Hot Tin Roof*) or **ARTHUR MILLER** (b1915 – *Death Of A Salesman, The Crucible, After The Fall, The Ride Down Mount Morgan*), though their work lies outside the scope of this guide. Other American writers worth exploring are EDWARD ALBEE, SAM SHEPARD, DAVID MAMET and JOHN GUARE.

JOHN WHITING (1917-1963) is less well-known. *Saints Day* (1951) is a haunting and obscure drama full of symbolism, and followed by a contrasting comedy, *A Penny for a Song. Marching Song* (1954) and *The Devils* (1961), a story of possessed nuns based on Aldous Huxley's *The Devils of Loudon*, are impressive. Whiting's early death robbed British theatre of a major talent. N.F.SIMPSON (b1919) wrote odd, absurdist comedies, heavily influenced by Ionesco. *A Resounding Tinkle* (1956), *One Way Pendulum* (1959) and *The Cresta Run* (1965) are of interest. HENRY LIVINGS (b1929) ought to be mentioned for *Nil Carborundum* (1962) and *Eh?* (1964), both illustrating his technique for developing characters individually in what he called "ten minute takes"

Censorship in the theatre was abolished in 1968, partly the result of the extraordinary, violent and sexually frank work of **EDWARD BOND**, who was a major Royal Court writer of the 1960s and 70s. His plays *Saved* (which depicted a group of disaffected youths who, among other things, stone a baby to death on stage) and *Early Morning* (a surreal comedy in which Queen Victoria and Florence Nightingale are having a lesbian affair) had to be presented to 'club members' only, and caused an outcry. These early Bond plays have a great deal of vitality and humour. His later, bleaker work, such as *The Sea, Restoration, Lear* and *The Woman* is magnificently theatrical if dour. Bond is an angry writer, with strong political leanings.

Another figure who outraged public opinion with his sexually frank and implicitly homosexual comedies was **JOE ORTON** (1930-1964), dubbed 'the Oscar Wilde of the Welfare State.' His precise, blackly comic analysis of his characters' self-delusion and questionable motivation can, at his best, become a statement on the human condition. Orton was brutally murdered by his jealous lover, but his work has hardly dated, though his outrageousness seems more muted now. His three magnificent full-length plays, *Entertaining Mr Sloane, Loot,* and *What The Butler Saw* are matched by some amusing shorter work, including *Erpingham Camp* and *The Ruffian On The Stair.*

The abolition of censorship led, initially, to a lot of outspoken language appearing on stage for the first time, and sex and politics being dealt with seriously and effectively. A new generation of socialist playwrights found their voice, several of whom have developed into very major playwrights indeed. Of these, **DAVID HARE** and **STEPHEN POLIAKOFF** have proved to be the most successful and subtle. Hare's important plays include *Plenty, Racing Demon, Murmuring Judges, The Secret Rapture* and *A Map Of The World.* Poliakoff is fascinated by trains as well as by politics, and his **Playing With Trains** and **Breaking The Silence** confirmed the promise of *City Sugar*.

Other important writers in this movement were **TREVOR GRIFFITHS** (*Comedians*), HOWARD BRENTON (*The Churchill Play, The Romans In Britain, Weapons of Happiness* and, with David Hare, **Pravda**), HOWARD BARKER, BARRIE KEEFE (a poet of obscenity) and **DAVID EDGAR** (**Destiny**, about the National Front, *The Shape Of the Table, Maydays* and *Entertaining Strangers*).

Few of these writers made it into the West End, for their work was too unsettling and challenging. Instead, the Royal Court and its Theatre Upstairs spawned the great upsurge in Fringe theatre, and the developments of several outer-London theatres, such as Hampstead Theatre Club, dedicated to producing exciting new work.

In the commercial theatre, though, there has been much stimulating work. **TOM STOPPARD** (b 1937) came to fame writing a play about two minor characters from Shakespeare's *Hamlet* in **Rosencrantz and Guildenstern Are Dead** (1966). With tantalising glimpses of Shakespeare's main characters, including a sight of Hamlet himself, the two courtiers 'sent to carry orders' are the perfect protagonists in a funny play about seeking identity. It owes much to Beckett's tramps but Stoppard's verbal fireworks make it rather different in tone. Stoppard has subsequently continued to explore philosophical and literary themes, coupled with a magnificent use of language. None of Stoppard's philosophical ideas is terribly original but the theatrical forms in which he couches them make them appear so. Subsequent plays include *Enter A Free Man, Jumpers,* **Travesties,** *Hapgood* and adaptations of Horvath's *Rough Crossing* and *On The Razzle*. His most mature play is **The Real Thing**, an exploration of relationships and, in particular, the nature of love, in which his verbal fireworks are less showy and more attuned to the subtly drawn characters. The construction of the play is, however, intricate and complex. Stoppard is one of the most important playwrights of the second half of the twentieth century.

ALAN AYCKBOURN (b1934) began his career apparently as a writer of boulevard comedies. It soon became clear, however, that there was much more substance to his tales of the aspiring middle classes in such plays as *The Norman Conquests, Absurd Person Singular* and *Taking Steps*. Ayckbourn's comedies have teeth and his observation of the foibles of mankind is extremely sharp, while remaining compassionate and truthful. He was, for a time, regarded as the modern Chekhov – technically his plays are superbly crafted and his characters three-dimensional and touching. This can be seen in the plays of his middle period such as *Seasons Greetings* and *Absent Friends*. Latterly, though, his already bleak view of humanity has become even darker and more disturbing, expressed in magnificent comedies which are more reminiscent of Swift than Chekhov. Essential reading among his recent work includes *Henceforward, Man Of The Moment, A Small Family Business*, and *Woman in Mind*, all of which deal with the breakdown of the individual in differing circumstances. Ayckbourn runs the Stephen Joseph Theatre In The Round in Scarborough and sees himself primarily as a director. Nevertheless, he has produced in excess of thirty plays and shows no sign of stopping. He is the most performed playwright in Britain.

BRIAN CLARK's *Whose Life Is It Anyway?* was a successful West End play with a serious theme – whether a man paralysed from the neck down as a result of an accident should be allowed to die. TOM KEMPINSKI's *Duet for One* concerns an eminent violinist confined to a wheelchair with multiple sclerosis, her apparently successful coming to terms with the disability shown by a psychologist to be a cover for a deep resentment and despair. His later *Separation* also dealt with disability, in a love story between a cripple and an agoraphobic. MARK MEDOFF's *Children of a Lesser God* (1982) concerns the problem of deafness, and LARRY KRAMER's *The Normal Heart* was the first play to deal seriously with AIDS, a subject later dealt with more maturely in **TONY KUSHNER's** *Angels In America.*

ALAN BENNETT, an exquisitely funny and deeply compassionate miniaturist, has emerged as a playwright of world standing. After the early comedies, ***Forty Years On*** and ***Habeas Corpus***, his work has grown into a wry exploration of the nature of the individual. *Kafka's Dick* wittily explored that writer's obsessions, and ***The Madness Of George III*** and ***Single Spies*** are magnificent, subtle pieces packed with fine writing and memorable characters.

BRIAN FRIEL, the Irish playwright, has finally become commercially successful in the West End, after a lifetime of producing quiet, subtle, moving and ironic drama. Read ***Dancing At Lughnasa, Philadelphia, Here I Come, Translations*** and *Faith Healer*.

WILLY RUSSELL may well be the best-known playwright in the land, after the phenomenal success of ***Educating Rita, Shirley Valentine*** and his musical *Blood Brothers.* He is a Liverpudlian and writes of that city with love and tremendous wit, creating superbly drawn female characters. His work appears to be straightforward comedy, but there are serious themes to his plays, and it should be noted that his two most successful plays are both versions of the Cinderella story. His other work includes *Breezeblock Park, Stags and Hens* and *Our Day Out.*

One of the most intelligent and civilised of contemporary writers is **CHRISTOPHER HAMPTON**, who achieved commercial success back in the 1970s with ***The Philanthropist***, a witty companion piece to Moliere's *Le Misanthrope* set in the ivory towers of one of our great universities. His career continued with *Savages, Treats, Tales From Hollywood, White Chameleon* and his hugely acclaimed ***Les Liaisons Dangereuses***, based on Laclos' eighteenth century masterpiece. Hampton's dialogue is crisp, his characters fully rounded and his sense of dramatic structure exemplary.

In the 1980s there was an upsurge of fine new writers, whose work is too close to us to enable objective assessment. However, it is clear that among our living writers, **TIMBERLAKE WERTENBAKER** (***Our Country's Good,***

Three Birds Alighting On A Field), **CARYL CHURCHILL** (*Top Girls, Serious Money, Fen* and *Softcops*), LOUISE PAGE (*Golden Girls*), LUCY GANNON (*Keeping Tom Nice*), PAM GEMS (*Piaf, Camille*) and SARAH DANIELS (*Neap Tide, Beside Herself*) are leading a new wave of magnificent female writers. Of the men, **JIM CARTWRIGHT** (*The Rise and Fall of Little Voice, Road, Bed*), **STEVEN BERKOFF** (*Kvetch, East, Metamorphosis*), MICHAEL FRAYN (*Noises Off, Make And Break, Benefactors*), SIMON GRAY (*Melon, Hidden Laughter, Butley*), **JOHN GODBER** (*Teechers, Up'n'Under, Bouncers*), RONALD HARWOOD (*The Dresser, Another Time*), STEPHEN LOWE (*Tibetan Inroads, Seachange*), **DOUG LUCIE** (*Fashion, Progress, Grace*), WILLIAM NICHOLSON (*Shadowlands*), BILLY ROCHE (*A Handful of Stars, Poor Beast In The Rain, Belfry*) and **HUGH WHITEMORE** (*Breaking The Code, Pack of Lies*) are all exciting, powerful writers.